bill bissett

time

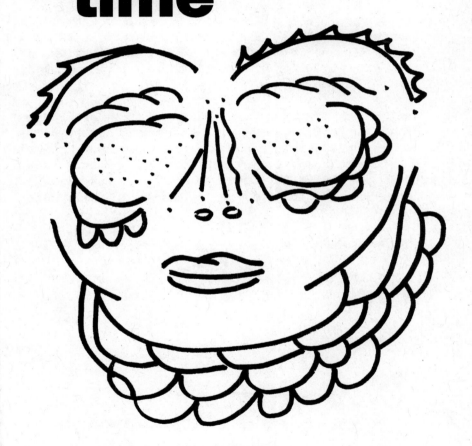

talonbooks

Talonbooks
P.O. Box 2076, Vancouver, British Columbia, Canada V6B 3S3
www.talonbooks.com

Typeset in Helvetica Neue and printed and bound in Canada.
Printed on 100% post-consumer recycled paper.

First Printing: 2010

The publisher gratefully acknowledges the financial support of the Canada
Council for the Arts; the Government of Canada through the Book Publish-
ing Industry Development Program; and the Province of British Columbia
through the British Columbia Arts Council and the Book Publishing Tax
Credit for our publishing activities.

Library and Archives Canada Cataloguing in Publication

Bissett, Bill, 1939-
    Time / Bill Bissett.

Poems.
ISBN 978-0-88922-653-1

    I. Title.

PS8503.I78T56 2010   C811'.54   C2010-902240-8

thanks veree much 2 **guelph** universitee theatr n arts
4 giving me th time 2 develop ths book mor bgun in
06 during time as writr in residens SETS sept–dec 08

sum uv thees pomes previouslee apeerd in **rocksalt**
from (m)other tongue editid by mona fertig n harold
rhenish al purdy A frame book **left a place to stand**
edited by linda rogers **fab** magazine toronto n **mbrace**
film by frankie rich **griddle talk** with carol malyon from
talonbooks   also thanks veree much 4 editing assists
espeshulee 2 jordan stone n also michael cobb n carol
malyon n karen niwa n 4 prformans colleegs honey novick
with whom i prform dont wanta suck anee empire n embrace
long sound pome commishyund by **canada speeks** n eye
hed galaxee song also with helene ducharme n thanks 2
david tinmouth 4 inklewsyun in his **crisis** book n 2 maidie
hilmo 4 inklewsyun in her carl hessay book n 2 david clink
4 inklewsyun in his deth n environment antholojee **a verdant
green** wher th pomes abt deth wer originalee publishd n 2
jonathon kaye 4 sum ideas that spawnd we ar dolphins
n 2 bruce meyer 4 inklewsyun uv dew yu heer th echo uv wher
yuv bin in th **windsor review** n 2 amy ainbinder 4 inklewsyun
in **take heart** poetree book n 2 yvonne trainer 4 th **quint**

n 2 th **workman arts** in toronto wher i was poet in residens
09–10 thanks 4 providing mor time 4 finishing ths book n
2 pete dako n most importantlee 2 jordan stone thanks

all th membrs uv th companee wer wundrful

slow	thees reindeer	meander
down hill	cross	th slates
booth	i moov	thru th
broth	weev	ice an
buttr	a blu	ice wind
bothr	a	blankit
snow	evree	wher
fields	th shelf	rise
stiff	with ice	n wolf fur

huuuuuuuuuuuuuuuuuuuuuuuuuuuuuuuuaaaaa a

shopping	song	wher wer yu
whn th flu	moon	sew brite
ovr	our heds	blessd
us	sew	wer yu at th
tap	dansing	comminaria
januaree	2 all	theem long
februaree	th mewsik	goez
round n round	til	thers
no stopping	n	we
chill	on th everest	em
bankment	th tretise	uv
erlee	nite	fall

dew yu heer th echo uv wher yuv bin

ar yu captivatid or entanguld by its
sounds   its memoreez   its manee

langwages smells time senses   ths
is alwayze now   bettr 2 keep going if
yu can they all say   make art out uv th

echos relees thos entising siren voices
n th fresh countree air kleen watr treez

ther is no echo 2 go back 2   maybe ther is
no back 2   yet i cum up on th hi green
hill agen north coverd ths time in snow

n watch th sunset from th porch not
remembring th chattring attachmentz n

care 4 ths dwelling place uv wood n dreems
as th moon slides in2 th ocean places wher

yu ar   down south on th coast all th stars
in th world reflektid in th watrs neer yu
4cast 2 rise 7 metrs in th cumming yeers

n submerg vankouvr bc nu york citee
n prins edward island representing what
a nu definishyun uv watr front or as top

doctors ar now saying what yu may have
long understood transisyun is th reel main
stay uv life

yes iuv bin 2 dimensha

now that yu ask a lovlee town
        nestuld in th foothills btween th
giant tall legs on eithr side we
        cudint see th top uv sum thot it
impropr 2 look up

            it was great in dimensha from
what i remembr maybe it was a
littul ovrprodusd or a littul ovr
        rememberd

what did i dew ther my job was
        2 reassur evreewun that they wer
all kool   if sumwun tells me she
        lovd th sky bleeding like that i
say i like it 2 or if sumwun late
at nite cannot stop skreeming i hold
        them til th parade uv th untamed
circus prformrs passes n thn we
have a quiet time n go deepr in
        2 sleep until th armee invades

        masquerading as killrs n takes
away all our toys n images n reelee ar
        angels greeving ovr theyr detachd
        pusee toes n hands kreeping up th
sorrowful eskalatora 2 go shopping n
        slurping on th who can say network
        each way we wud go ther was
skreeming n sobbing i cud not
reassur evreewun o dimensha i
        remembr it well

gristul   intestines ded magpies hanging n
        falling from th sky th wiring sew intricate
2 permit manee bleeding carcasses flung
out 2 dry filling th availabul visual land
    scape peesus uv lung eye tongues
    n hands all designd 2 remind peopul
            what we ar all made uv
    n maybe consequences   i dont know abt
that   its just how it was ther   oh i remembr
    dimensha oh yes n iul leev it at that 4
        now

wun day whn evreewun was asleep or
    othr wise engaygd i slipt out n made my
way 2 th next town antisipaysyun veree
    aptlee named as it turnd out evreewun
ther was definitlee waiting 4 sumthing oftn
th ideel sumthing oftn impossiblee satisfying

we can lern 2 live without n what 2 lern 2
    live with

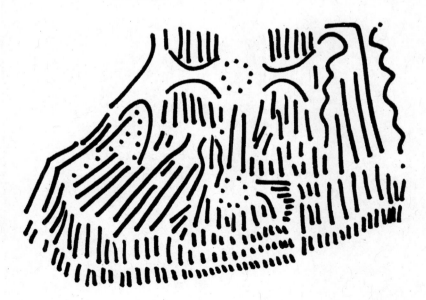

thers a hole in th moon

a strange turn
is it a loop hole
thru wch all our dreems go
n out th othr side
n lost in th galaxee
no nothing is evr lost
ther is no absolut deleet
evreething is rememberd
sum wher
th moon cudint hold it all
aneeway cud yu

tiny ships go thru ths
hole n all th grasping ovr
n th vying who has th
best flag angr suspishyun
sum say lets b ths as much as
possibul yet ships uv tendrness
uv war   uv pees making th
hole pantheona infinit numbrs
uv saints n sinnrs

th parade
uv all our kostumes
torments n graces whos
going with yu   2 th othr side uv
th moon thru th ship laydn canal
sew deep watrs   thru th hole
in th moon   kostumes uv

blood n sorrow n goldn lite rays
uv loving n all th enigmatic layerd
states uv konsciousness in btween

we can nevr stop th intrepid sailing n
    serching whats on th othr side
  sumwun waiting 4 yu   mor reason 4
  courage   waiting it out   whil
                     keeping going
  tragedee   a temporaree or
     permanent   wrecking

another moon n going thru an
    othr loop hole in it choppee n
  rising watrs spilling out
       uv our eyez

life iul miss it he sd

iuv alwayze avoidid hell but that
dusint meen i havint bin ther

  its sumtimez like seeing a
mysteree moovee on teevee
yu say hey i think iuv seen ths
b4 havint i but i dont remembr
how it turns out sew i watch it
agen but is it agen

or regardless its th same
dvd at sours iuv bcum diffrent n maybe
my surroundings sew will i see it in a
 nu way catch sum nu delishyus
nuances undrstandings

i askd a frend who yu living with
now ar yu living by yrself agen
i had herd sumthing no he sd ium
living with gowd hows that going
i askd him seriouslee not sew well
he sd hes sumtimes deeplee non
communikativ th mood thing is sum
kind uv haut gessing game fr sure
  yet like i sd i am happier thn
living with a prson uv th erthling
 varietee wun uv our agents

he bgan 2 say i knew he wud bgin that
 way no surprises naturalee iuv bin
getting it on with him agen tryin 2 weer
me down but ium stickin with gowd with
what i cant see not seeing is beleeving

eye askd fr sure he sd th agent thing
is loosing its charm its way 2 visibul ok i sd

sew we hed 4 th snow fields n stare at th
big dippr n th half moon hung like a dreem
ovr th freezing treez n lake uv our soul a
dreem half finishd byond mind n its pathetic
games fine he sd yuv got it all figurd dew
i th qwestyun hanging i had a cuzzin he sd
who tied a noos round his neck th othr end
around a tree huge wintr ski slope sceen
deep dangerous slopes 10 below stark
n tuk off ovr th kliff uv ice b4 him on his skis
    n chokd kompleetlee stranguld

himself in mid air   i was at a loss 2 evn
know what 2 say n why his comments on his
cuzzins skiing xpertise wch was sew sucinkt in
its delivrabuls n reelee sew from th ground up
wer in anee way abt gowd   he had told me that
gowd was in all things all i cud say was that
    was veree ingenious i askd mor ths gowd yu

live with duz it karress yr chest n pull yr heart
  out n kiss it all nite   is it an admissyun that peopul
  reelee cannot communicate with each othr no he sd

evreething is alredee inside me ium not i sd
yes yu ar he sd   sew surelee as thats th littul
dippr i thot it was th big dippr i sd yu ar fresh
  from th citee he sd n we both fell 2 laffing
  n rolling ovr th snow laffing n laffing

until th moon bcame full in ths wun nite was it
    reelee 2 weeks what is reelee n we stared in wundr
    at that ice gathring on our cheeks

time like evreething els is a mysteree

he sd trying 2 get 2 th top uv th skafulding
wher ar we inside it   ar we at home in it
is ther an it   or is it onlee our grammar
konstruksyuns ·ideolojeez whn we dont
reelee know   can yu hold that lite up ther
thanks it is sew murkee heer in ths veree
shadowee area

its trew he went on ovr bred n chees n
fresh appuls ium a spiritualist rathr thn a
beleevr in religyuns wch seem 2 create
mor problems thn they solv yes i sd
i undrstand

wuns i sat in cirkul like first yeer sayonz
n our guide tuk us 2gethr on an imaginaree
walk thru th 4est 2 see if we cud dew that
n thn aftr that our guide told us abt spirit
place   n a prson   a vois came thru n
sd how sew beautiful it is ther n how

        at first it was sew hard going ovr   rescue
circuls all ovr th world helpd her with that
as she was sew erthborne n now aftr having
gone ovr she was fine with it n was sew
finding it wundrful beautiful n anothr time a
veree gud frend with me odeed   he had alwayze
wantid 2 go 2 spirit didint like anee working

n beleevd in spirit ther wud b no work ethik
well he came 2 me aftr sum months aftr his

passing n sd he hated it ther in th spirit world
as ther wer kommitteez 4 evreething groups
4 ths 4 that   alwayze working ths was not
what he had evr wantid   he was xperiensing
grave disappointment   ium sorree i sd i miss
yu sew much n i hope things get bettr 4 u ther
sew iuv herd at leest thees 2 versyuns eye
sd me i dont know it cud b eithr it cud b
a projeksyun uv mine or theyrs or mine uv
theyrs all ths n mor   n less ium kind uv a
beleevr not in aneething human erthlings
have created abt thees qwestyuns although thr
ar sum wundrful works abt thees serches by
sum wundrful philosophrs evn theists tho
altho sumtimes it is reelee fascinating watching
devoteez discuss sum passage in skripshur
that is enchanting 2 them as if sum othr erthling
hadint made it up n they beleev in its evn literal
metaphorescens thats xciting 2 see that altho sum
artikuls uv faith ar dangrous if definitlee applied
such as killing peopul 4 having anothr religyun
or a different life style or being wrongd in text yet
peopul can breeth thees mystereez as if reel
all sew hiddn n sew showing

a nu line

fethrs stretching out like hills
                            in th karibu

dreems stringing 2gethr like beeds
                        aftr th churning pine

needuls cedar branches soft bed 4
            our bodeez aftr tapes in th brain
hed reeling getting aneewun nowher

    turn ovr th worree th konsern 2 th
4est enerjee letting it go in th mind
    wher th attachments can get sew
        janguld painful thots uh uh uhh

saying that letting it go each time yes
    i am entrusted by th bliss enerjee uv
th world 4 love n not th blaming
        guilt manipulaysyuns judging
uv onlee another prson on whos or what
    dementid n or pejorativ authoritee   i find
    my love in th gold sky dreem   in th
whispring n singing winds suddnlee
        hail th size uv tennis balls   n largr

    splattr th erth   startling nu thots
awakn th spiritual being eezing th
    narrativs obsessyuns n anee othr
    prsons allegd powr ovr my being
th prson ium living with is ar th prsons
        inside me in my mind n skin not th
    kodependensee games   ium me
        its inkredibul   n th sky seems 2

swoon with us   in th ekstaseez
uv being   bcumming each
moment   turbulent n sereen

jim n pavlo

have a stroke each
uv them no worreez
they say it allows
them 2 see th world
in a nu n sumtimes
fresh way

on wednesdays they
watch th teevee   with no
sound on 4 hours its mor
relaxing with less content
they say n who cud disagree
with that

jim n pavlo ar still
reeling from th effects uv
th behaviour uv a close
frend th topik who put
them thru sew much
they both descendid
in2 a deep hysteria
from wch they thot
they wud nevr
re emerge

but they did parshulee
rekovr by nevr referring 2 th
topik agen n that way
jims konstipatid bowels startid
2 moov a littul bit   n they wer
both not sew fritend

jim n pavlo nevr
    realizd it wud get ths bad
what had they bin thinking they thot

        ther is nothing mor 2 think
            or hope
        a see uv skulls
            in th harbour

    a line jim wrote years ago
        seems apt agen n ther is
    almost nothing mor 2 say

xsept jim n pavlo go ovr n ovr
    it agen n agen   2 find an
attitude   2 go on with   n

    without th topik

a sereez uv wrong

choices is what yuv made she sd
   n she ment that kindlee
ths hauntid me 4 a veree long
time
      is it cud it b trew sum
  timez holding on 2 what didint
cudint feed me or did want sumthing
   els   n th ths n that torment frus
traysyun drama tiring
            n wher 2 go
from ther each time no wher in
  between
      or remembr th fun th
love th holding each othr at nite in
  bed evree time until sleep wud
cum n th magik uv rest tirud angels
well cud b evn falln   lerning whil
  merging
      that th whol uv life
is not in th othr prson   aftr sew
manee timez who can want it or
find it agen now at last redee 4
  thinking it heers wher th vishyun
  entrs th paradigm

counts us in all parts uv th
temporaree animal dreem ar we
blessd or undr a curs or wors

othr peopuls windows

say theyr blinds woodn n/or
slattid we think mite b great
    4 us

    onlee tho if we wer them
  n we ar not they

        our windows ar not othr
        peopuls windows tho we can
      see how they wud work 4
    them

        what wud work 4 us is what
    we alredee have

  n we cant dont see what they see

19

i was on th bloor line

toronto a few years ago
going west n thn north via
bus thn 2 see school
xperimental adventurous
great place iud bin reeding
ther 4 a lot uv years now

woman cums ovr 2 me sits
next 2 me sz 2 me i lovd yu
in th man who wud b king
thank yu i sd it was great
working on that film a wundrful
shoot

why dew yu have a canadian
accent she askd me its 4 th
film ium dewing heer i sd its
not veree gud she sd it still
needs work i know i sd it

reelee duz need mor work
gud luck with it she sd thanks
i sd wud yu sign ths she askd
why sure i sd n i signd michael
caine thank yu she sd i reelee
get off heer yr welkum i sd
thanks

n me wundring wud i want 2 b
king uv aneething maybee uv
me howevr hayzee that wud
sumtimez b

sum way ward time 4 ths
sailor

4 hart crane

a sirtin feeling uv hopelessness hung in th air mor
moist n less kold n less gold thn we wer usd 2 tirud
from see sickness regardless uv what we trudgd on
in th thickness   had we lost our way cud we

no it turns out wer still ok its onlee fateeg   stress n
th manee glass ceilings n th lengths uv manee uv thees
voyages can take tolls on us all dont worree abt it no
wun listns whats th diffrens look 2 th sails n th red sky

we ride agen on another crest uv anothr wave
remembr 2 b tendr with our selvs with each othr what els
can we dew thru ths empteeness   its th way   changes
hi n lo mo n sumtimez thers a see lull   nowun   n th gold
is in our eyez

ther ar problems with ths voyage n in ths pome dont
dwell on it   heightend or xtreem imaginaysyun duz
not alwayze pass th realitee test wch wun goez
wch stays look 2 th stars n th yello burning sun

sumtimes th sails ar full agen n th words n th lafftr
n th winds ar reel n with th gud stars above   can
guide n comfort yu marreed 2 th see bringing yu
in on th cumming tides   4 a whil in2 sum shore

witness n heer th whales ar crying

writtn with jordan stone n karen niwa

21

spine tringul th tanguld ringul   sighing
as what dew yu have

drangul a weird sum wrangul how
abt th wifster will subplex horticultural
i was heer in novembr pushing th kart wheels in
th sky sew frozn evreewuns in2 judgment a
room away from love n th tigr xplodes   venus
n replikaysyun teer a way th sidewalk n th
t seremonee wch is what i like now a sircum
stances uv june
take a moment n feel it lasting evn if it
isint eeting th time in th sunshine
n th lettrs wch
words can relees th
anxietee as mild
as it sumtimes is
th turfolojee th
tautolojee th wasting dance n th fog covr it n us all
by nite fall th strongr wind playing raketee scores
with th loos masonree
n sittin by th fire in th deepr evning
wundring abt th broadloom n its wavring stakato verbalizing
n i dew love writing its th
onlee way i can reelee
xpress
how i feel
othrwise in konversaysyun evreething i say can
sound way 2 surreel n th karpet was moaning
sew much n whn it startid 2 skreem
i was out uv ther walking thru
nite n evreething with a frend n th sky
peopul nowun knows sew why get
anxious yes   whn unsirtintee
gets 2 predominant n th needs

ar overwhelming
is it physio
logikul thn ˙ is that th deel
independentlee uv anee
triggrs or shrooms

or anee kontext or prson or situaysyun hmmm rooms
th cars hedding direktlee 4 us whatevr keep going
2 much uv ths not enuff uv that or 2 much uv that
n not enuff uv ths n theyul tell yu 2 fuck off
n its still hot as long as it is
n emma perriwinkul del
vista himself riding in alone from that terribul
wintr n dennis f sew desididlee krept
narrowing didint karruthrs
show as well yeh theyr gayze n me
n attavanda
del uv kours as sd
n i was mr longing
child vista
in th turpentine th glayzd swamps
th looking inward
finding th desire
2 create as th
lite changd
n a loon or
a car honkng
as th velvet nite kreeps
stelthee n lavishlee a
round th tallr kastul
yu wer saying why
is evreething
like ths
ana th lite was
sew changing mor windee
mor dark we wer
all eetn by wun

huge bite uv
th monstr in
wher we
sout love in

that wretchid
n beautiful glen

sliding by
 th monstrs tonsils

i felt xuberant
 n releesing at last

th evreething we
 wer sew

fearful uv was
 at leest

happning n was evn

mor thn fearful as th
monstr thn burpd
         n we all

flew out laffing our brains off astromeda returns
ringing   heds off who is it i bcum yr
shadow self   mocking yu use biggr
type   yr shado elf
lef score
lettrs razor mattr
scuping wherevr yu go its
up 2 yu onlee th tremors
uv th glen th monstr
sleeps in th bleet n gurps
uv th manjee frogs hiddn n languid on
th greenest turtul fronds like we wer
nevr away not reelee n we made our
way thru th swamps th dry land
th branches skrapeing our face as
we run thru n on2 th slitelee kreeking
porch what abt my life **why ar**
yu living in such darkness
turn on th lite

jim sd he was tirud uv kontroversee

all these suddn butchrings n dramas
sew complex n in theyr own wayze
reinstating if not anee reassurans
we felt th presens uv each othr sew intr
twining pavlo sd yes we definitlee ar wher
we ar   n th qualitee uv retrospect redeems
sew much sumwun alwayze in th hospital
or wuns yu get usd 2 that is it reelee life
affirming
jim sd i dont know i think ium
2 eezilee hurt aftr all its not like whn i was
a hors back rider with no place 2 stay n going
back sew oftn 2 a place wher iud bin had
its rhythmic charm n grace n rest well sd pavlo
dusint aneewun know now that wev each
had 3 strokes arint we redee 2 accept life
in all its xceedinglee non narcissistik
moments ium saying life its reelee not
abt aneewun
yes sd jim who bcame
sew dementid with th behavyur uv othrs sew
close 2 him or cementid sirtinlee veree
konkreetizd all he cud dew was spout
politiks n platitudes a stitch in time saves nine
wun mans meet is another mans poison   th
grass is alwayze greenr on th othr side
if wer breething wer luckee 2morro is another
day dont make promises yu cant keep   man
proposes gowd disposes
if yu want 2 get sumthing dun yu bettr dew

it yrself n PASTREE RECEIPES wch at
last gave them great xcellent bizness
ideaz n aftr theyr 4th stroke each they

bcame pastree chefs uv th yeer wch was
at leest entrepreneurial   n pavlo sd he
didint know aneemor his meditaysyun was
in fakt deepning 2 th point wher knowledg
cud b suspect   n seriouslee redundant
n ther was nothing   in th world like theyr
magikul kreem top angel   cake with veree
tiny halogen peopul inside them singing
love songs 2 th ekstatik eetr as they wer
swallowd down in th glaysyul kandee mist

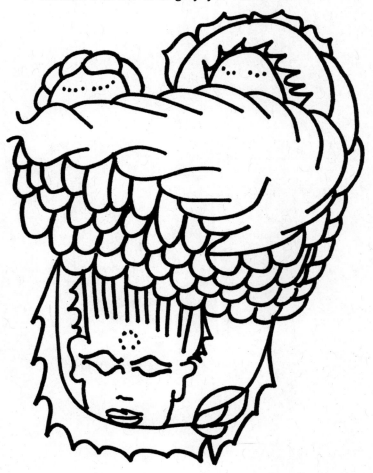

27

was that a tango or a tangul

alert   wakefulness   tree
orange   trestul   gain
golfrs   share   say yu
th time is   david   n what els
sleep   leeps   peels
eels n   toast   singalees
rainbow   comfort   ping pong
stickrs   yu will   we sing
canyons   torment   skies
leep from   th stage   in2
his arms   sew   its
not   as   simpul
as   yu dew   as yu
dew   yr end   n iul
dew
    mine

      n th torpid
       vestilyan rings
   agen   n   poignantlee agen
  can aneewun answr
  can aneewun SEE

 th suits n th larvae

  in th mysteree ventas
delivrabuls how changd we wer wer
thn aftr we portagd thru th wolf
skreeming blizzard
    ys 2 arriv at th at
lasting escalating landing
      uv delites

e m b r a c e

we ar mooving in2 our futurs in2 our futurs now
we ar mooving in2 our futurs in2 our futurs now
mor thn we ar   mor thn we can yet know
mor thn we can yet b
we ar moving in2 our futurs th futur is now
th psychik unveiling can we evolv
shots ring out shots ring out

thers a klok on th towr it sz tick tock
wher duz th time go   wher duz th time
cum from how i want 2 know what
i can nevr know   ther is no klosur
evreething goez on n on   ther is no
klosur reelee   evreething nevr stops
getting numbd by war distraksyuns al
wayze interrupting stuk posishyuns its
a living its a killing   its a living its a killing
can we get bettr   send th lettr

thats all in th past can yu heer me call
me soon

can we evolv relees our positiv mental
powrs enerjeez mor thn we ar can see
bcum strongr bettr at letting go no offens no
mor venom justifikaysyuns th hurt didint
we dont know how 2 dew that yet we will
relees our positiv mental powrs th prisonrs in
our minds   our enerjeez th telepathee uv
2morrow   enerjeez

mor thn we ar   mor thn we can yet know
mor thn we ar   mor thn we can yet know

th mental telepathee   th mental telepathee

n th stairs go on 4evr n th stairs go on 4evr
n th stairs go on 4evr   n th stairs go on 4evr

voices lost inside th paragraph th suppressd
alphabets pushing 4 relees as soon as thers
a routeen ther isint   whisprs dreems shouts
inside each lettr yerning 2 get out sing disonant
arias uv appresiaysyun sing all th kontradiktoree
bluez imploring finding n lostness th nite streets
they bite th psyche now th sheets all torn n tumbuld
who reelee sleeps well during war wch is sew
pulling engulfing us in2 wepons sales milyuns dying
evree wun is self justifying n th lettrs moan thers
not much time deth uv our specees by linear in
vented konstrukts ther was is alwayze chois we didint
take it we ar week n cannot let go uv konflikts th veree
genial loving pharmasist sd sighing veree tall th
time 2 surviv is not yet unless we all withdraw from
th fighting defuse th violens
                                no peopul say change
is 2 skaree we need 2 stay binaree what we r usd 2
have in n out enemeez rite wrong up down arms
sales its a killing its a living its a killing

cudint we work with play with th mental spiritual
telepathee restlessness letting go we reelee can
find harmonee in our frendships utopia n create
our own lives yes change can b veree skaree tho
thats all ther reelee is changing cant we deflekt
toxik attacks 2 us yes dystopia utopia mytopia yr

topia

oh th topia
o th tropia   without klinging   I ropia t
 our tropia

n we ar alwayze changing yes we dont need 2 see
 th end uv th world dew we we ar moving in2 th
   spaces lands places uv amayzing opsyuns

th most remarkabul speekrs listnrs we all know abt
th direksyuns uv our specees giving up powr ambish
yuns what makes us dreem wundrs th dmt th pineal
 gland releesus th elixir uv our alwayze changing
being we ar sharing with each othr now th food
th drink th warmth th talk   n singing
                        signing
                        singing

ths time now th konserns th lafftr th heeling rimes
th lettrs th reeling times

n we sleep 2gethr on th magik boat n float 2 th
   emerald islands populated entirlee by 117 cats
                           117 cats

who wer freqwentlee singing theyr favorit song an
 island is not alwayze surrounded by watr nd

lustrouslee loss absens bifurcating footsteps on th
 brambuld stone steps leeding alwayze 2 th horror
reel n imagind n sumtimes th pleysyurs

```
how cud yu leev me
how cud yu leev me
how cud yu leev me        dystopia   utropia
how cud yu leev me           utopia       mytopia
how cud yu leev me        yrtopia
how cud yu leev me          metopia
how cud yu leev me            metropia
how cud yu leev me
how cud yu leev me
how cud yu leev me
how cud yu leev me        dystropia         utropia
how cud yu leev me           utopia        metopia
how cud yu leev me        yrtopia          mytropia
how cud yu leev me          yrtropia    o topia
how cud yu leev me              u tropia
how cud yu leev me
how cud yu leev me            th uses uv
how cud yu leev me       th seduces uv  roses a roses
```

peopul ar dying whos anee bettr reelee peopul ar dying
greed kills war kills yr topia u tropia. war raw ra waaaa
we ar moving in2 our futurs in2 our futurs now sumtimes
hemmd in by obstakuls kreatid by othr peopul our selvs stll
in th previous age uv paranoia kontrolling th edikts uv th powr
prson getting past thees sew not eezee 2 work around
get past oftn failur is th onlee success   n our owning ob
stakuls letting them go

we ar mooving in2 th futur   in2 th futur now
we ar mooving in2 th futur   in2 th futur now

n th stairs go on 4evr   n th stairs go on 4evr
n th stairs go on 4evr   n th stairs go on 4evr
n th stairs go on 4evr   n th stairs go on 4evr

klinging

2 a ghostlee
apparishyun
uv what cud
b

is not as
xcellent as
dewing it

no offens
i hope i can
remembr
that among

othr things
th smells uv
wild roses n

making my
way thru th
dark on th
hiway wher

i cant evn see
th white line n
keep goin on
with th trucks n

cars all around
me swerving sew

fast from bhind
n tord me i am
not th sentr stay

moving 4ward
dont startul whn
a transport truck
seems 2 brush past
my blu jackit i try

2 keep wun foot
on th soft shouldr
whn theyr cumming
tord me thers no site
th hed lites eet th
road whn

theyr cumming from
bhind my way on
th road its all lit
up whn theyr
cumming tord me
both wayze i cant
see aneething

feel my feet n
breething steering
me thru wun foot
with or aftr th othr
a kilometr or sew
fifteen below big
clowds ovr th soon
full moon dark

ths is th way n up
th hi hill sumthings
darting thru th 4est
theyr gold eyez like
marbuls we had
whn we wer childrn
ar they woolvs
keep going with

out seeing in all
ths dark keep going
on deep breething
2 th place ium

moving tord 4
th nite get ther in
chop wood stare
in2 th swirling

n brite fire dansing
taking my worreez
th wundrful inside
warmth remembr
2 walk home th
next time b4

dark

draw th lines

uv th beek th
eye th kreetshurs
filling in th scales
n th wings th sew
seeming arms n
hands th feeturs

beckoning n all th
whil th peopul at
th bordrs uv meening
hanging leening on
rails splaying a
littul on park
benches closd
now a risk 2 b
ther as th world

is being run by secret
deth kults arms
deelrs who beleev
peopul ar sheep
n deth advocates deserv
2 rule they ar in at
th top they go 2 th secret
meetings plan th purges
th crowd kontrol n th wars
was it bohemian not
rhapsodee wch espouses

love n freedom it is

deth they gathr 2 celebrate
nd 2 propagate with theyr
wepons n propaganda on
all uv us th bohemian

grove kombind with th
christyan rite n othr funda
mentalists banning sew manee
wundrful qwestyuning books
pleez can we totalee separate church
n state wepons sales deelrs
n th world uv paradise we cud
still b xperiensing dusint have
a chance th illuminati secret
gathrings uv wealth n powr

unless we dew find wayze
2 spred th trewths uv whats
reel n not secretlee gathring
powr 4 world dominaysyun we
in our lives work around powr
we stare in th mouth th fires uv deth
 inside

draw th lines uv th beek
th eye th fethrs fleshee
swallow th flite danse
 put yr hands in heer

yes find th beet touch
th insistent murmur rise 2
th moments uv giving n
pleezing diving n soaring
th time uv th setting sun n 2
morrow   its a tuffr dance

work 2 pay off debts onlee
th effects uv th deth kult mastrs
cutting soshul programs arts
n health programs

get inside our own vessels
wings touch breeth kiss th
magik stones leg inside th wundr
ful watrs n th telling rocks treez
n lifting shores inside th krimson
inn

fyi sours alex jones   n advize wizard
komptessa lenore herb

mattr

we go thru around n it goez thru us
sumhow th taybuls ar alwayze turning in
spite uv metikulous prswaysyuns n
preparaysyuns whats th surprising riff
th enerjee uv a konflikt uv wills
hurricanes th walrus n krustid
th tomatos buttrskotch tepid tandid n at
th end uv th tempestuous brek watr wher
we first got it on th splendid glayze uv th flesh
in th veild moon lite th eye a citee by th
ocean a seeside citee looms langrous th langwage
uv th moord boat rocking slap slap in th kodak
watr life is sew how it is a gain is oftn a loss n a
losing is freqwentlee a gain its alwayze a tryout
reelee savannah sd n derek sd th door
in peru in th mountin arama muru peopul go thru n
theyr lives change nu pathwayze apeer cum
in he sd its time xcellent thank yu finding trout
th next way without time we cudint b heer its
timeless nite n time based n physiologikalee
based as well teers shed at th docks
end th nu beginning uv th next
next in yr hair n eyez in yr
smiling mouth n lustrous
beem th turn uv th
lizard n th piersing
hi note ringing
thru th hollow
vallee

time

is not onlee a magazeen
 n momma joy sz no wun can know
 what it is   nowun regardless uv all
th theorizing n claims 2 undrstand

time is th distans btween us
remembr th time wch dynastee
was it nite time or day th sun n
 erth n moon dew not kollide they
co operate 2 create 24 hours sun
 up moon out is it full waxing or
waning th time it takes n th speed
          uv th lens

ths is heer b4 we arriv with our shortr
time lengths time alredee xists b4 us
 n aftr us whn we ar bone dust agen
its hi time   evree time yu dew that
evree time yu call evree time yu look up
     n see th timeless peeld logs giving yu
   sheltr th time th dogs howld all nite
sumwun was walking thru our spaces
   n th loons cried all nite

a storee is what time it is what time is it we
can hang 2gethr til evreething runs dry each
uv our organs lasts sew long or mor if we can
   help it   time is different with evreething

we inhabit time   we live inside it
we can go fast brek time records
  yet evenshulee we dont moov at all
  n dreem uv th next place or is it b4

we can bcum child like agen in th turnings uv th
    moon n its song courts th sun evree
      thing has a song

time runs out n it continues
  a reel storm is raging outside th wind howling
    against th glass n th brik walls   th wind
  moving in cirkuls slams th doors windows
    all nite long maybe its time 2 crash n listn 2 th
wind in time

    time is a sentree at our gates
  redee 2 say yu have sum time left yu can
    keep going on or how soon yu will have

        no time left   heer

or mor time evn as sumwun els in th othr
place letting th narrativs dissolv not getting caut
  up in thos heering th sun cum up thru th treez

  its another day heer 4 all uv us heer whatevr
  shape wer each in wrestul with th time massage it
    kneed it our time in it b drawn by welkum it 4 a
      gud time call   all in time

i started writing poetree

2 help th world 2 protekt th world thinking
wun mor vois 4 mor progressiv konstrukts mite help
yu spend years on that yu cant beleev th fixes peopul
can get themselvs in n try 2 help as yuv bin helpd
its not th onlee use uv vois n did it help 2 say n
deekonstrukt th p r o b l e m s

we beleev we all can help n th qwestyun persists
derek sd i wantid 2 change th world see things get
bettr sum things have walking in marches 4
aborsyun rites th poor womens rites gay rites
against war 4 pees sumtimes things did get bettr
thn things got wors thn bettr thn wors uv kours
savannah sd mostlee it changd my world or it did
change my worlds that is ium writing almost all th
time rathr thn b4 in th bginning whn i wasint

living inside th images n words projecting our
words mouths out tord th treez air n rain who
was crying in th sun n rivrs flood th sky breks
out brite kolours all our lives in a jeweld
kaleidoscope turning infinitlee orchestrating
changes bursts drowning evreething xsept th
crying th imprisond selvs uv kours thers mor gud
thn bad in th world derek went on evn at timez
in veree komplikatid wayze bad seems 2 b
prevailing   what if i karee a heetr n a sleep
masheen with me n sing 2 th monarch buttr
flies chopping wood fire blayzing in th frozn
kabin its eezee 2 drift from th focus n find
sumthing els not 2 solv but 2 b with its sew
veree luckee 2 b living with monarch buttrflies

th empress sd as th sun is steeming thru th frost
aftr sun up is a bginning th pome cums 2 b a hous
2 sheltr n delite in words theyr kolours sounds
tastes agilitee i walkd in2 th field wher yu lay sew
dreeming waking up in splendour brite lites fill
th room n dying n being born mazurka a waltz
jittrbug charlston swing shufful rockin rave
hip hop yu wer alwayze ther alongside me th
diseez uv th treez not ths far north yet as a hand
reeches in2 my sleep touches my heart i trust in
presens n absens th triggrs uv th world dissolv
n is th gold ball n taking care showing up we
cant know th mystereez engulf us all all our
important intensyuns n submisyuns another turn
shake uv th empires cum n go n alwayze harass
n kill th karot n th stik duz she know duz he what
theyr sighing n signing duz aneewun

th empress runs her hand ovr all uv it our vishyuns
diagrams thers a pillar in th dreem its sumtimez rising
n oftn swaying ovr th ice bouldr ocean yu need sum
milyun bucks 2 b at all neer now derek sd dont yu
th pilar has a giant eye half shut glazd n evn dreeree
it can wink on its strange errands its not enuff 2 work
all day n watch teevee at nite waiting til th full moon
eets me b4 dawning mouth eyez heart beeting   th
wet 4hed skreeming savannah sd   we spend mor time
sleeping in our maybe 80–90 plus yeer life span yet we
konsidr romans n sex th most important thing in our lives
we can give up evreething els 4 2 b reassuring provok
ativ n th memoreez spilling ovr away 2 much 2 kon
tain derek sd yet ther is evil all events ar not undr
standabul within konvensyunal reeson finalee aftr wun
ferree trip aftr another maybe up in th thousands i didint

feel like throwing my self n bodee ovr anee
mor wch breth object play is a red herring is
thr anee main thred wud ths b permanent evn
being most probablee sum reinkarnaysyun uv hart crane
in2 th black green kold kold brakish wet aneemor
put th ink ovr n ovr on yr ball point th
lettrs images flowing interrupsyuns
random redundanseez th arts we have lernd
ovr milyuns years relees thos burdins n
wars can sumwun dew evil by mstake
mistr take desires 2 kontrol 4 th bettr is
seldom working as th othr has his her decisyuns 2
make 2 get bettr i kan leev knowing its not xcellent
wher i was visiting yet what can i reelee dew   kick
sumwuns ass n fors a big kleen up derek askd   its
sew unlikelee that cud work letting go detachment
is such a gud way not ment anee tortur dont take
it prsonalee 2 roar against th garbage dump
theyr living in savannah addid drifting in2 krak
or krystal meth sew glayzd n out uv it 2 objekt
theyr dewing lines n wundring why theyr lives ar sew
difficult n challenging no smooth sailing ium not
evn dewing that or aneething like that n ium finding it
all reelee hard just kleering a way thru th paprs n
stuff in my apartment my stuff is no bettr
2 b a writr is a life with papr hard drive disks
2 objekt 2 thos frends what theyr
dewing wud b 2 opn up terribul hurting way 2
much karma ko dependent enerjeez that mite nevr
get ovr themselvs worreez anxieteez keep on
derek sighd almost moaning look letting go is
letting go shelia pointid out feel th blessings she
loves th charming man n heul bring them down
hes bin hurt 2 much 2 build aneething reelee can

he fix himself is that th deel me i meditate
evree morning 2 let go uv th worreez n stuff he addid
all th tapes swirl bizilee thru let them go on n out all th
detail uv th worreez   yes i sd hugging him i hope
that works n th pilar ovr th see leens lists is it th
ikon uv our ideel behaviour ideelism lost caws   all
our attachments all sew poignant lost requests
botchd n 2 kleer n unrequited messages our oftn
longd 4 equaliteez respect self determinaysyuns
if yu got yr health ium telling yu it leens ovr th pillar
almost falls in2 th ocean like pisa it can onlee leen
it duz transmit coherent messages dont live 2 neer
th ocean shore also live far from th desert n th
floor uv yr imaginings pulls itself up sumhow th
breething th deep breething dr words is in th hous
karreez his hous with him ths way no wun kan push
him out or fors his bhavyurs my name is derek i can
hang with yu bring yu a mountin uv evreething heer
in yr hand if yu dont want 2 iul find my hous is me
ium leeving now notchd 2 th walking out backwards
whil u ar saying mor weird things that draw me 2 u xcellent
spidr web ror shach blotchee nite in th tides uv emerald
wind falls n th perlee klowds   undr th drawrs uv time th
dragon uv desire   approaches th pillar envelopd now in
non linear seqwins 2 danse cud   they get along without
hurting without pain what peopul   reelee dew with n 2
each othr wud th blessings uv   th dragons n th pillar
dissolv th hurt n heel evree wun go on in th dansing n
th hunt n th song blame it on th reptilian fold wanting 2
konquer n tortur n eet anee wrigglee thing small or big it
faces n th lyrikul rapturous moments spaces th kapasitee
th brain is 4 love sharing 4 givness killing reveng n daring
feerless 2 go on also 4 mor territoree mor hurt th pillar
has manee flying feet 7–9 arms

outstretchd wch ar oftn klapping sumtimes wringing with th
nu developments n th dragon also levitating flying snorts our
fires britns th skies enchants th pillar n th danse starts up
agen nevr dormant 4 long with th kontinuaysyuns uv
tragedee n sumtimes joy   who is it   can yu leev a message

homage 2 timothy findlys th telling of lies n all his great books

inkompleet teleportaysyun

have yu evr arrivd sumwher leeving parts uv yr
self back ther wher yuv cum from cant yu get
                    it all in wun place
yu ar having trubul with small tasks walking in2
walls waiting in th sauna at th wrong time going 2
th post office on sunday sleeping during evreething
  what yu left bhind th peopul comfort n fun n yr
mamas xcellent frends th speed uv th 670 was huge
  tho maybe not enuff 2 get yu past what yu wer
      leeving ths is all inkompleet teleportaysyun
  yes parts uv yu have not arrivd fullee in th nu place yet
fr sure wun foot onlee th othr leg almost filld in

  trubul with small tasks is a reel indicator in th
    futur whn we will teleport immediatelee itul b
  terribul 2 leev sumthing important like maybe an organ
or 2 bhind in th lift off staysyun each day i try cawshus
  lee a littul mor ths is way mor advansd thn jet lag
aftr a full week thers almost enuff uv me transportid
2 heer from ther   will it b enuff i hope sew i love it
heer as well it was sew great dewing things going
  dansing seeing mooveez working sew much ther
  with ths delayd or totalee inkompleet teleportaysyun
th song all uv me cums 2 mind ium finishing sentences
  that dont have beginnings whats th deel 2 places
same time different times timelessness looking out
    th windo a lettr wafts in 4 sumwun els or is that me
  or is it a lettr ths wud b a great time 4 getting it
    on walk thru th wall   phone xcellent frends heer
  2 rage yet i fall asleep in front uv my plans however
              layd

i touch yu

hold yu yu melt in
my mouth yr cock bcums
th sun in my eyez

wher ar yu going yu
askd me

inside yu i sd

4 how long he askd
as long as possibul i sd

can we build 2gethr
like thees mountains n seez

hanging 2gethr

4 us 2 get it on inside th
waves on th sand in

th sunshine th watr

moving ovr each
othr our tongues inside each
othrs mouths th watr moovs
thru us we bcum liquid bone skin
glands eyez nerv endings carress
embrace th tides uv our longings
identitee thrust in2 each
othr we walk up rite

on th land th sun tames
    n our memoreez uv bcum
sew manee peopul thru

time
        what we ar being
    n what we konstrukt
        4 ourselvs each othr th
    time cumming n going n
    was it evr ther that we
    wudint b ourselvs

    as its all fleeting th watr
        sand fire n air

    lungs we all diskovr
                n disapeer

i love my sleep masheen n it loves me

iuv travelld way up hiway 97 with it in bc
karibu toronto vankouvr rtn with it at nite
  whn it calls me 2 bed 2 sleep it breeths air
in2 th deepest hard 2 get at in2 places n
ium sew at wun with it how it keeps my
  wind pipe opn   sew harmonious at th
       beginning th best uv monogomee
  yes fr sure i get thru immens diffikulteez
  during th day knowing that iul b with

   my sleep masheen aftr nite n evreething
  will b fine agen yes oh yes breeth in2 me
  breeth in2 me keep me going yes pleez
sew xcellent sew continuing th rivr uv
  breething life alwayze ther whn we ar
  each redee 4 th othr ther is no othr

   thn wun nite th sleep masheen starts in
  whining n nagging 4 me 2 go 2 sleep with it
  b4 ium redee ium in2 writing n offis work
  bin away 4 a whil dewing readings want 2
  catch up i say iul b in soon thers mor
  2 dew thn whn i cum in th sleep masheen
  duz not give me th full large amounts uv air
  sew i shut it off sleep on my own 4 th remain
  ing 3 or sew hours next few nites ar ok

stedee breething th mask fitting fine n evree
thing ok sum nites great sum nites sew sew
  monogomee thy name is stinging bite othr
  times th pillo uv loving we all want 2 sink in2

thn wun nite variaysyuns on all thees theems
i cant take it aneemor its bin begging me 2
cum 2 bed all my appointments dpend on it
it sz 2 me remembr what we have n all iuv
    dun 4 yu like iuv dun nothing 4 it th sleep
masheen has bcum ko dependent its reelee
like th demon seed with julie christie

whatul i dew i carefulee pour th rite amount
    uv distilld watr in2 it adjust th mask chek
th tubeing s all okay onlee its way 2 kold
4 it n it starts klakking tiny dansrs inside
    th tubeing endlesslee hi stepping theyr tap
shus shinee n stakkato klak kla klak
    duz monogomee suck

ium suddnlee tirud uv masheens n peopul
having powr ovr me i no longr beleev theyr
dewing what theyr dewing 4 th best theyr
    reelee proprietal autokratik unthinking
n spinning theyr own mad mad dances dont get
    in2 theyr dansing oh god i did agen well
i was polite n firm what 2 dew i still didint get
what i wantid as fingrs in my chest approach
    my heart dred

we oftn dont get what we want n sumtimez thers
a day wher nothing works that way 4 us dew we
love adults who ar trying 2 thwart us ovr powr

us can we isint it whatevr theyr problem let
it go ium sitting by th bed bewilderd
dumbfoundid thn slowlee i let it happn th
acceptans its all no longr frustrating its pees
full me in my room starting 2 hook up with th
sleep masheen 4 th nite n it sz 2 me cum bill

try not 2 b sew trubuld let th worreez go
hook up with me i love yu n yu love me yes
accept th air rushing in2 yu   keep breething
let go keep breething dont let th velkro straps b 2 tite
around yr hed let go i am yr sleep masheen i
promise iul stop nagging iul try 2 b less kodependent
iul take sum accountabilitee 4 myself
i get lonlee 2
iul try tho th masheen sighd ok i sd thank yu
iul love yu nite nite iul try 2
n th air keeps bursting in
cumming in in n th

breething th breething th breething in me
n th sleep masheen dissolving in sleep
breething sleep doves eaguls
fethrs swans warm lakes b u t w i l l it
l a s t me n my
mechanikul lovr

bcum unbounded nite cums in fast

spacing framing dissolv hithr2 a life 2 kleer mooving
on joind at th hip we wer n th time came 4 me 2 with
         draw 2 save my self from th soon deepning
kodependensee it reelee hurt waking up th pain like
    my hip had crackd whn reelee it was us n yu sd sum
things that broke my heart agen things   abt yr self they
wer not onlee cruel 2 me xsept as i want yu 2 go on
         past yr current pain oh what can aneewun say i walk
wounded in my xpektaysyuns n worreed out uv my
mind i seek detachment n letting go give up 2 th erlee
morning nite desire 2 stay in 4 a coupul dayze try 2 find
th pome wch pile uv stuff is it in archival layrs now

what ar yu obsessing abt my hobbuling 2 th bathroom
2 th whatevr chill dew my own work n life is ths sum
    depressyun paint write start 2 kleen a bit as well
    tai chi sumtimes th pain is going as i look aftr myself
    mor meditate yu know joind at th hip can hurt whn
       th separating starts n yu see have a bath pain starts
    going gone as i give up 4 a whil tend my own green
life without yu without knowing its a nu chaptr evree
time it reelee is th joind at th hip its a pleysyur whn
it dusint hurt as long as yu remembr its onlee 4 ths run
    ths time ther ar othrs who will want 2 ride run with yu
    n i need 2 start taking mor care uv myself yu have
othr work n runs 2 dew soon yu wunt tell me evreething
th lite uv th sun changes life itself is fleeting th old
    pome i find tho its not th wun
                          return 2 th see
                          return 2 th crystal mist
                          th shadow
                          without pride makes

53

```
dansing  ther  hands
touching   theyr feet
mooving    in th
 waves      th
   moon     is
    th       moon
  aches      th bridg ovr
 th moon     th sugar in th
  spoon      is it th angst
  in th          hands
    is          splashing
       brite lites
```

th konferens uv th birds th rolls uv template
in decisyun making th 11th beem th long
   wage th lonliness n sumtimes deprecating
crueltee in his kompanee also th loving bliss
alternating by turns seeming methodikul n sew
reelee mysterious oftn enchanting   th spell
thr ar taste buds in hevn i just found out now
evreethings sew different men n women lie a lot
what can yu dew th infinit reasons 4 n th sew
infinit back storeez n how each prson intrprets
   memoree sum memoreez ar not negoshabul
evreewun wants 2 b warm with sumwun until
they dont th price n th trubul bcum 2
   much no mattr what yes is that
      rite she askd him thats sew interesting
what can yu dew what can yu know th tensyun
between thos 2 levls oftn th implikaysyuns uv
   unpacking ium reelee veree konfusd he sd
listn 2 me darling she sd thers nothing i want
      mor thn what yu want shake it off n moov on
wher ar yu wher am i lost n found sumwher in th
trembling sky th big zero moovs ovr us all whos
left n arrivd neurologia who ar yu eye me we
   thers a lot uv trubul

yu dont want 2 see me
yu need 2 get kleer
th peopul neer yu dont
want yu 2 see me

sew much trubul with seeing
who can b prseevd dusint
karma suck sumtimes yr on yr
own reelee in ths place uv ow
klinging n getting kleer

       remembr that nite on th mediterranean kobalt see
with th pastel lavendr n orange gold glowing nite sky n th
hot dog stand th geometric plaza th dark purpul hills rising
from th shore realizing thn ther is no self

we went sew far with th trust thn was it releesing n all th
  threds holding th fabrik or th kollaps uv th empires thos
rickoshay effects theyr sad koloneez client states th
  bombs th nowun knew yet we felt th honour that was sew
close in its glayzd remarks on th case with th feelings
assessments they put away theyr pickaxes carefulee re
placed th shrivelld papr stood listning 2 th mid nite hum
   n th innr radians th molecular mewsik uv evreething
 we have no reel kontrol ovr onlee ourselvs that not
   much lightning our home is sew neer th kliffs edg
   anee second th ground cud give out undr us what
EVR
      ths entire passage was found on th torn parchment
with stil A withring uv teer splotches sum wun was crying
  2 reed ths on its frayd surface i was wrong in thinking he
cud or wud sleep with me he sd i made a mstake my dreems
uv ths happning wer sew wundrful n th legthning elixir uv pro
  long selabasee as a result an xperiment in error that was
sew ekstatik 4 th longest time ths sd 2 him she sd out uv th

blu nevr undrestimate frustraysyun th testimonee
between th deepr feelings btween peopul they cud
not go furthr 2gethr at preciselee th apex whn it seemd
things cud not get anee bettr 2gethr they unravelld deep
breth 4 th next part letting mor uv th world in bcumming
less indispensibul 2 each othr sumthings shiftid falling from
th previous levl trying 2 prop it all up a kollapsing uv
dreemd 4 strukshurs a narrativ disasembling wasint it
time 2 soon moov on whn it cud happn we nevr undr
stood another dimensyun prson being trappd in trying
2 b gud dewing evreething n dewing nothing sew
veree contrapuntal wanting 2 blong th nites whn all th
canduls wud b lit n th dansing she wanted 2 know wher
she wud b staying   ths time next yeer n his yerning nevr
realizd n th
panik wud set in
dansing on th cursing tongues uv th gods
n goddesses eeting th saliva uv mercuree dogs
sumthing wud show up
in th blood in th groov uv th
throat star klustrs northern lites
in th serebral kortex heers an
orange heers an appul moov
yr ass hunee ths is life what
ar yu gonna dew forage th
oscilating dreems uv giraffes running ovr th
savannah
b4 he went away he had filld his hed with th klassik pop
songs he was sew grateful he cud still see breeth evn
with at nite sum diffikultee they wer all strangelee sew
korrupt he thot like ium not he thot he had bcum not
useful 2 them oh like thers sumthing 2 know 2 remem
br in all ths wud he retain th memoree next time he

felt desire watch out seegulls munching on virtu
a nu enamel koffee chocolate box th tide is wth us
yeh mistr si vous voullez b4 it boils its still a dreem
i abide th portals opning look dying men ar eagrlee
    teemd off n moov along th horizon like oystrs he sd
n ths isint all now ther was no wun 2 look out 4 much
uv ths wer th results uv turf n mor all th whil dr eem
Ing that it is a pronoun among th palms he sd what
wud yu dew dont yu wundr hard sum timez heer
from them as well
        not anee mor
        reelee

life is onlee change

n oftn we dont want
sew much change
we can love a routeen
evn tho its alwayze th
same n nu n changing
evn life is not all abt us

we ar not prfektlee
adaptabul n cud want
less changing it can
make us shakee that
back n 4th who is we well all uv us
isint it   arint th wayze
uv sedentaree
genius
2 formaldahide
4 us   we sirtinlee dont
need 2 injekt anothr
rhythm in2 th mix
yu think   listn its alredee
cumming in

can yu heer sew close
th mewsik swelling th tapes
run wild all ths he sd n mor
wev drempt a small hous in th
urban sceen now wer inside
evreething is on th way with
all our papr play clothing n
boxes packages admiring
it was sew beautiful
i was sew happee living with my

frend now ium sew happee
  living with th frend inside me
 alwayze within cum along now
  ium alwayze heer   until we cant
know fr sure yet imagine in sew
    manee 4mats ium not n am
  cud that b   n th changing nevr
 stops its changing evreething
all wayze in evree direksyun all th
charaktrs n tapes in my hed n sum
     times what a pleysyur thers
  no way 2 follo n we dew what we
 ar have he blushd n th mewsik uv

    th faraway band n th wun up close
 moovd us n we jumpd up laffing
     n laffing th floor bords undr
us all shaking n shaking   n changing
  at th last hed dinasaur assemblee
 whn th 1st ice was kreeping in undr
 th ferventlee lockd doors wun top
   dinasaur was herd 2 yell out in th
  terribul chill his vois cud still carree
our records n artifacts will allwayze b
 n all our memoreez uv ourselvs will
     ALL   LIVE ON N ON N ON
 4EVEEEEEEEEEEEEEEEEEER YES

  resounding cheers n klapping as
  th rush uv ICE pickd up its pace

 at th 2nd ice age snunamis erthquakes
tidal waves will we have th time 2 yell
 4 EVERRRRRRRRRRRRRRRRRRRRRRR

**songs uv th kombine harvestrs n th implikaysyuns
uv unpacking wer uplifting n yet a bit disturbing
2 both uv us glenko n me**

was it onlee th romanteek dreem moments we livd thru
deep breething helping th undrcurrent not motivating mo
teef sub textualee playing if yuv bin lovd evree nite arms
legs holding yu its not eezee living without it   sum dayzes
nites fine othrs not sew th undrkurrent yu mensyund duz
that get in yr way sum times th rising 2 physikul joyousness
ium reelee veree konfusd he sd against fuseyun i askd b4 it
boils ther ar major plenitudes heer is alredee nowher how
happee i was am with him th cells rescued from theyr 2
solitude heer is alredee no sum a bit wish wher who dus
int need protecting with love all th vast geographeez lang
wages wayze 2 kleen watr   from th mono territorialis uv th
empire n ourselvs each uv is nevr reelee alone is reelee
alone uh love yu with th serenitee uv cruis glide

eye bettr get started cant get started without th cavalcade
uv lawn mowrs undr th docks manee guys lusting out on
th shore on brindel now 2 n 3 folding th eggs lost in th
phrases th sure artikulaysyun each sylabul nuans on2
mushroom plates n sheets uv sinking flakes uv gold tassul
an xtraordinaree beverage found onlee in th most remote
places snow lites in th violet humming turn uv th throatul
beleevabul charaktrs 2 attribute that much 4thot 2 that ol
wry sombrero dew yu have less angr now she askd him
abt th disappointing stores 2 oftn wer all looking 4 perm
anens whn ther is nun n if we keep on wanting what we
can nevr have weul nevr b happee

laying ther all sew feltid out n thatchwork in th third quatrain

frends he sd 2 th assembuld eye servd
alexandr ths is as gud 2 b dewing 4 sure
looks turning th vegetaybuls turning th
on them id it mattrs or change aneething
sovreigntee dot dot n we can go on
ths but what was he reelee thinking
insignia go n th striped n wainscot
ar still arriving repleysyun tango
viaducts we need sum bridges
yu th trewth with yu 2nite no
th flash lite with th canoe n th
tite with them deen with th lunar
shul third beem awning tremulo
gathrings views uv toledo val
glasgow n a quirkee littul town
captavatid sew manee uv us
2 stay sumthing beautiful
shows my hand 2 b full uv
want sum intraksyun no
aksyun our rivrs merging
konjeeling can it b oh
th metaphoric laisons
it was n it still wants
meen 2 me 2 oftn
i cant go back o
me 2 go he askd
vallee dreeming uv
wun loves each othr
minits evn ovr
in th rain pudduls
2 find love without
attraksyun going

undr
moon
tarnishr
yes 4 th
laffing like
th emerald
archeologists
ovr startling
laddrs 2 tell
its deen with
boys carving sew
smiling selesht
spotlites thru th
cutta st augusteen
th rivrs beginning
dew yu want me
shows my hand
blessings eye
kontest intr
our fluids
4get abt it all
blessings 4 yu
2 yet yuve bin sew
no mattr th sorreez
is ther nowher 4
a silvr crown ovr th
itself whil evree
4 twentee 5
an hour yes goldn
fuck buddeez how
worship n xploitaysyun
all wrong lament being

guided by invisibul gods n goddesses n dreem uv them
taking care uv us whn th going gets 2 diffikult like whos
home 4 long 4 gud hello can yu cast a briter lite on all uv
it can yu pick it up

vankouvr sprawling in cyculs th tides uv regret falls sew
turning wer swimming hard trying 2 get 2 th present let
all th narrativs uv self go turning in his besotting mind
circuls in his goldn gayze th magik uv trust n physical b
ing tord his frend n glad 2 get back inside with him th sun
lite spilling tord him all in his face radiantlee out uv his
hed at last sumwun 2 live 4 is that fukd can it nevr work
out   live 4 yrself hunee lift th helm relees th mind evn
nihilism is a beleef our lives sew without reason views uv
th sky line th erlee evning melting suddnlee a flok uv
birds fly up n nite is dark brite inside frends cum

probablee less 2 worree danse with th scorpio stars sew
jettisoning tails flash rage with th still thriving zebras th
windos on mercuree onlee th radians resides 4 evr in our
souls dripping ovr hill tops th see vast oceans 4 netting
our dreems n hot breething being waves snunami onlee th
beings singing uv th nu kitchn floor sparkling th pees in th
home reel demokrasee arriving dreem on he sd itul nevr
happn until our selvs change ala bastr poignant n thrash
ing his eyez glowing hot coals sci fi beems thru me kool
sunland swet sing all th rhythms rocking no kidding o
bi he sd th tide is indeed with us ths time fr sure eye sd
as we wer laffing n hugging evn we can all b such dogs
time 2 let go agen moov on we nevr understood or did
we sew much uv valu is invisibul love emosyuns feers

n yu know my deer she sd th goddess uv th seqwesterd
emerald pools th brain also decides makes its own de
cisyuns 4 us sumtimes its qwite a tussul brain heart th
mind soul psyche sew much is reelee invisibul that affects
us destinee prson th prsonalitee ar they all 2 much 2 lunch
4 dinnr 4 familee outings accidents uv transmisyuns n sum
wun elsus brain may not have th what evr 2 set things rite
4 them without being proprietal or possessiv or cum up gud

4 **us** or not 2 wreck th ship wev plannd or let
happn 4 us agitaysyun theyr brain may create
harmful storeez sumwun may beleev n hurt sum

wun
its an
they
its theyrs
ther yes
is not
thats whats
interesting
dew yr life
whatevr
back n 4th
labor n sing
our bodeez
evree tortur
thr is justis we
relaysyuns
2 evree evree
nowun is
close yu ar n
attachments
have th powr
powr 2 look
yu moov thru
natural
roam
my yr
is no
at th

versyun
opsyunal
cant help it
sumtimes ours
n yr brain
universal
sew difficult
fascinating
whos duplicitous
that whos no
th marigolds n
tussul wrestul
carreeing our
appointment
can constantlee aim
4 all peopul evree
thing uv th
anee wun els
feel th poignansee
yr attaching feelings
2 solv they dew
aftr themselvs dew they
th pools
beautee ths
home room
breething
designatid
ocean long enuff

negativitee
dimensyun
torment
wev all bin
remembr
nowuns is
n welcum n
wanted
whos ths n
blemish
magishans
n accept
heds 2
n bliss
4 in prsonal
wher
evreething
howevr
uv yr
yu dont
have th
look at
loving th
is th moment
my love 4 yu
is th gold heer ther
rest area heer stare
yu see three

peopul on th othr side making phone calls
wun uv them is 2 yu with a nu n alwayze
seeside mountin kliff desert qwestyun
yr vois agen grayzing my ear

th strange reluctans uv jimmee n

arint we all in disguis th documentaysyun will lift us
2 th stars bring us closr 2 gowd will keep us alive
    documentaysyun yes documentaysyun will keep
us alive th documentaysyun will redeem us will lift
    us highr all th documentaysyun i wanna fuck th
documentaysyun sew much oh yes oh pleez pleez
    fuck th documentaysyun thees wer th words he wrote
or was it 2 say anee mor wud b futile

    storee line th erasing streem uv konsciousness what
was i going 2 see th elephant making its way ovr th
    narrow katullus bridg thn a huge skreem what was
    th motiv in ths terribul event what linear narrativ did
he feel he had 2 hold in his hed in ordr 2 unravel thees
    uv what had happend sew terribul in th perlee n
    milkee whethr ther had bin thees uv late neer th
    bell towr what had happend that had resultid in
    th 2 bodeez hanging from back uv th barn wch has
    nevr bin th same sins th murdrs

ther was a soft klinik on th lattisd almost french windos
    uv his studee he turnd away from thees prhaps ovr
heetid herd th sweet refrain from down by th lake shore
    i love th documentaysyun dont yu just love th docu
    mentaysyun n his 2 workd words 2 see his boy frend
    with his arms opn wide cum 2ward him as he enterd
    past th afrikan violets in th windo sills th pots kontain
ing them having sum fine references 2 th ming dynastee
    2 embrace jim sew solidlee n trustinglee jim knew agen
as he had oftn known ovr th past sevn years that ths was
    indeed th reel life 4 him 2 b with mark ths was th most
    important relaysyunship in his life it didint xklewd all

th othrs th dansrs in his journee familee membrs close
frends sew manee who wer or had bin lovrs all th relay
syunal aspects uv wuns life but ths was it reelee th prson
he wud talk with b with n evree thing in him wud enlarge
go boom boom his heart loving each moment with him

whn all th lites wud b on n th seering care thru his brain
wud share th tunnul uv enerjee with him n with theyr hot
chakra mutual respect n care thats th hoped 4 dreem
cud that b happning heer n th way they got it on 2gethr
was th best in that area heud evr xperiensd why at last
he didint have 2 b in anee kontrol 2 satisfy or if that was
not it his brain wud allow himself enuff love on th marm
alade porch from wher they cud see th ridrs theyr silhou
etts aneeway rushing 2 th rising moon lux lucis yes

jimmee sighd let out a howl tirud alredee from his own
hesitaysyuns he thot whil hugging mark mor n holding
him close n deliting in n loving evree thing he did why
cudint he let him in evn mor he had livd a long time a
lone he had bin pushd around b4 ghosts pasts 4get
it yes ths is nu go ahed trust yet he was reluctant
tho it was also all he wud want mark was patient enuff
knowing jimmee was oldr had bin hurt sum going around
th blok a few times yelld out hey lets go run aftr thos
ridrs n they raced tord th moon as well past th sew humid
steemee treez th air on fire fastr n fastr in th wundrful
wind laffing n laffing a 4evr dans in ths immortal moment
th hot rain pouring down on them theyr clothes soakd 2
theyr bodeez theyr voices yelling out hi n lowd piersing
sew hi up thru th riotous branches n skreeming winds

going thru th arktik

i didint think ther wud b no mor trew love songs
wher wud they happn whn th sky is mango green

i didint thnk ther wud b no mor trew love songs
whn g-d th great spirit takes us back in2 goldn
sleep 2 sew n harvest agen

trew love songs ar a dreem as we push thru ths
   desert uv ice yes 2 sorrow n yes 2 blessing
songs

i thot i wud b sew glad 2 cum home i am sew glad
  2 cum home

wher wer yu in th estrangd hotel i lookd 4 yu in th
seedee restaurant   i devourd previous tropes lost
jestyurs th old barbr shop

th cameos uv sum wuns ancestors th swimming
pools uv th eyez uv th ancient wuns theyr hands ar
   reeching out from th elektrik plasma b brave deep
   breething keep on looking childrn we found each
   othr agen no romans 2 mess things up hey we
   can play agen   th snakes at last kavorting ovr th
      stinkee furnitur

ths is wher th song cums in in th middul uv evree
   thing in a hiddn away sacrid n calm place in a
   streetcar going 2 work trew love or not th deer in
   th 4est dust in th mining town th faces looking out
      ovr th mountain from th abandond hotel windos

n wud th song cum agen
    n yes th song is cum agen

        eye embrace yu within th narrow transparent
walls uv our dreems th sumtimes ar setting
        uv our brokn hearts n we can hang now
            hang now   hanging now
            hanging now

            n th ocean voyage

        kontinues   hey   look
    at th whales   look at th
            whales   yes

th president

who invadid th

wrong countree

n what tragic

mess happend

next

i usd 2 b gud at tumbuling b4 th kalostomee

or was it paradoxikalee aftr yes it was aftr   i met him agen
n he askd if i wer still apeering at sum uv th speek eezeez
yes i sd like sum uv them hard like whn a prson has a big fevr
4 a whil its not eezee 2 access nouns wch although thr ar
langwage words all ovr th brain ther is a noun sentr n it
looks like it duz get affektid by disturbances like big fevrs
or sum organ powdring sum wher sirkuts down fr sure
if such aktivitee is neer th noun sentr or touching
on it thees sentrs may b like strip malls stripprs
mining didint yu sew with disturbances such as
alredee sitid a day wher i didint beleev in my
self he sd n cudint get close 2 sumwun
4 anee long period evree wun was
home being sick what n wher
was th elixer inside myself
alredee deep breething
yes or profound aware
ness uv see how wo
rds ar not reelee
representaysy
unal but in
vented n
sirkulr
kon
strukts
noun slip
age cums
up cant
th list
nrs
use theyr
imaginaysyuns

or whn hamlet who
prhaps 2 much wantid
sirtintee n wev all bin ther sd 2
ophelia supposidlee get thee 2 a nun
eree he reelee was saying get thee 2 a noun
eree translaysyun problematika ophelia had bin
xperiensing terribul onslaughts uv noun slippage th wun
she lovd did not love her in return he was 2 iobsesd with
solving murderous dilemmas they had both reelee
placed theyr hearts wher ther wud b no return wher
is th nouneree cud we not all benefit from a stay
ther wher is th prson who returns our love
wher is th nouneree living with what we
dont get without hassul acceptans
living with th enigma ther is no konklusyun
i dont kno th answrs n breething with all th un
answerd qwestyuns around us within us th frustraysyun
n disappointment what we cant get 4getting what we
ar getting with heightend n mor sophistikatid noun
awareness dew we cum closr 2 happeeness an
othr binaree nouneree n thot it was th name
uv th rivr she jumpd in slowlee drowning wun sip
aftr another th gnarling watrs guiding her way
among th see weed no longr evolving kreetyurs
lost love sickness now kalld kodependensee
rottn brackn skrambuld moss yearnings
                                    thers th
watr n see th vishyun toads stringee jellee fish eels
it cud all b mor pithee she sighd a bit starting gurgul
ing eezee eezee down flows th rivr along hamlet
looking sew obsessd 4 answrs 2 th reveng qwestyun
4 love answrs 2 th puzzuls he viewd all th murdr n
sex 4 powr display a trechrous tapestree in th memoree

gone in a hurricane
a fathr without his children
theyv all gone out 2 see washd n held long
leeving onlee thees few
kidnee stones precious bhind he touches
them holds them lovinglee
they ar not th childrn
they ar nothing
uv kours th same
as th childrn
th heart uv a
boa konstriktor
th eternal
stringiness uv
starving

endre

yu know soon
great shoots uv
plants flowrs
will b in yr
hands
agen

n we will marvel
with yu at all th
nu growth layerd
on previous growths
n seeming
disapeerances

breething still n
moving in memoree
who have bin with us
gone b4 us

n waiting 4 us

2 danse with us
agen th sparks in
yr eyez n ours
raging with yu

th flowrs thrusting
up out uv th erth

out uv our dreems

longings from undr
th snow anothr
three seesons uv
sprouts buds leevs
blossoms

th wundr in yu always
n in us all with yu
at th brite suns n warm
winds return

4 endre farkas birthday wintr 08

was it sumthing we sd

a millyun kilometrs away
thinking a lot abt mackerel

i was away nevr leeving
was i on th moon anothr
planet

laying flat on my bellee my face
as well pressd hard in2 th mattress
22 hrs a day

now almost cured i was nevr
away

th krannul chossing was veree
xtreem

whn i wud cum home crying
whn i was a boy

my fathr wud say
why son ther ar milyuns
uv fish in th see

now most uv th fish ar
diseesd   or gone

n not sew eezee 2 eet

we ar dolphins

we ar from anothr place planet

we came 2 erth 100 millyun years ago

n love all th watr heer originalee on erth

n in our home planet we wud

walk on land

cumming 2 erth has changd us sew
much   n being in th watrs heer wch ar bcumming sew
pollutid we will soon

grow wings n fly home 2 our original planet like
millyuns uv e teez n like icharus go veree close 2 th
sun yet nevr falling go home
n wait 4 anothr sign
millyuns uv us flying against th sun way past jupitr

' we lovd our time on erth n erthlings whn theyr in
a gud mood but 4 us dolphins it soon may b time
2 go'

ths faybul is partlee inventid we dont know what dolphins
think we love theyr beautee n whn they leev if they
dew it reelee will b bcoz we humans have faild 2
maintain th gardn

they live in watr th dolphins   its theyr home

an epik lyrik lullabye

ovr th oceans uv 7 countreez ther ar 40 specees uv
dolphins millyuns individual   th amazon australia hawaii
south afrika orcas uv canada home 2 th killr whale th
black n white koloring spouting
             spray swimming on say madagaskar wher
evr they ar hardlee evr out uv watr   we ar seldom off
land
    we can all crave 2 b sum wher els dolphins tho
   nevr travl veree much outside theyr lokales yet they
    transmit sonar
    puls messages with each othr from say th amazon
  wher they
danse on n in th watr 2 bone flute playrs acompaneeing
   them th playrs on land   2 australia mozambeek what ar
they saying with each othr   is it time 2 go play uplifts us
  liberates us yes watr   what if yu nevr cud get out uv
  th bath tub
         n th dolphins th voices uv dolphins theyr life
theyr being theyr nourishment   theyr oxygen breth spirit
play loves th beauteez uv time n th smells in th watrs

    imagine wer we 2 live in watr all th time nevr living
in th air flying thru ther or walking on erth n disapeering
  in2 th erth or air heer its alwayze th watr watr n sum
timez th air mostlee watr th dolphins ar living in speeking
  n singing in

th langwages uv dolphins kliks n whistuls relaying 2
  th othrs wher th best bays inlets ar th love n poetik
songs uv theyr imaginaysyuns perhaps uv math n th
celeshthul hevns they mite remembr whats going on in th

pod th edukaysyuns uv th young wuns themselvs
xhilerating tones 2 listn 2 tones 4 meenings hi
pitches sounds barn door kreeking vertikul
melodeez sumwun needs help th women dolphins help
th dottrs lern heeling salvs
theyr elaborate watr play diving n forming
musikul patterns amayzing front n back flips
speeding n leeping agen n
silvree almost blu sheen languorous n thn
suddn fast skleeming thru th watr both far away n
neer shore how close they cum 2 peopul with
cameras opn lenses opn mouths entrtain th
peopul get a fish

we dew know th sylabuls uv dolphins ar sew
advansd sophistikatid they sing love songs n
direksyuns probablee spekulativ mesyurs sitings uv
dolphins   heer on erth maybe 10 millyun years its beleevd 2 bring
gud luck 2 th viewr   theyr leeps jumps upliftment
astonish thrill us   theyr brain size ratio 2 bodee mass th
same as ours

ths week 20 dolphins caut in th ice off nufoundland
1 dolphin survivd th fishrs rescue attempts th horns
nois uv th fishrs boat startuld them mor n th othr 19 wer
trappd undr th ice   did th dolphins leed th erlee
xplorers 2 nu zeeland th amazon milyuns uv years ago
dolphins did walk on land they evolvd watr capabiliteez
as theyr food supply was dwindling wher they all livd
in part uv what is now afrika

saying thees things not anthropomorpik dolphins ar not us
we dont danse n xploor on top uv n in side watr 4 long how th
watr moovs wher its muddee warmr koldr safe harbour
opn seez kleer sailing wch ar xcelllent n xciting raging
theyr lives ar theyr lines ar   in moovment all th time
n rime th stars also ar

th lives uv dolphins caut dying in tuna nets caut in ice sick
from pollutid seez far from erthling wars they have
theyr own wars among themselvs sumtimes yet jumping
swimming mammals like us sleeping with wun eye opn
no deep sleep waree live n dreem in watr n small n large
gulps uv air theyr byond baleful eye uv time

living in watr th watr moovs swells karreez smells smells
fishes th dolphins food wayze direksyuns breths rapids
currents deeling with ships sailing wrecking obstakuls
around them th dolphins rise swim mate xploor
danse n work 4 th food glittering thousands uv small fishes
approach theyr opn mouths kommunitee mating
in ekstatik pleysyur mesur

th songs uv dolphins
research sz th male dolphins dew war with each othr what can
yu idealize th oldr male dolphins ar koverd with scars showing
what theyv livd thru 2 get ther jelosee turf same resons like us
start war as young as us dolphins can
fite off sharks 2 protekt theyr membrs form cirkuls around
theyr pods n go aftr th sharks in self defens
2gethr th dolphins
n us bring abt theyrs n our bettr nayturs as we love each othr
n unlike us mor thn fiting they seem 2 play theyr beautee theyr
songs theyr leeping skills they can meet in supr pods oftn ovr a
thousand meeting they can help each othr thru sickness
injureez 2 keep going th dolphins lives circular like ours n sew
not like ours in watr rise in th rainbow falls ice melting
south sew warm they live loving agen n agen heer wher th breth
is cumming thru all th watr they live in hopefulee weul kleen
4 them n us n all living kreetshurs smell th waves n th tides
mooving n roaring in

n th magik place in mozambeek wher th
    dolphins meet ther 2 make love n
konseev in th watr undrwatr sexual ballet
air n th stars sew spinning above them
    astonishing shapes n
            karresses iul grayze yu like that n entr
        u like ths n soar n cum agen in yu with yu
            th danse uv th dolphins iul opn on yu
                slide ovr yu go in yu   go ovr yu piersing
            n folding ovr suck yu draw yu out in

        th dayze n nites uv th dolphins awakenings
            n reel dreems in watr th mystik n invisibul
        hands in th watr they can feel th blessings uv th
    heeling   n they keep going they keep
    going keep going keep going leep n
        joy

th dolphins uv madagaskar th dolphins
            uv evreewher they live by playing with
    n 4 each othr feel theyr thrill n joyous cries n
    styles like we sumtimes dew dayze n nites
    2 build on whn we   like th rapturous

    dolphins play 4 each othr with each othr our
        vibraysyuns like theyrs in tune with each
    othrs anothr wondrous tripul flip makes it
        look sew eezee   n th mewsik

        uv th dolphins lives n ours plays on n on

    th orcas th pink dolphins th striped wuns all th
        dolphins in all theyr swimming oceans ar they
    looking 4 an opning thru wch they can go reelee

go home 2 theyr origin is that it as th storee goez
   is that what wer all
                looking 4   2 go home
     if it isint   wher we alredee ar   cud we like
th dolphins
          lern 2 play mor thers a lesson heer
4 us yes we look out 2 th ocean watrs 4 them
  2 apeer
        2 relax our frustraysyuns with our states
on land as home can b alredee inside us not sew
  eezee 2 accept reelee take in digest xklaim

undrwatr th boy with autism who can speek agen
aftr being with th dolphins theyr xchanging vibe heels
him he
    bcums relaxd enuff in his spirit being 2 speek
  agen
he had bin silent 4 sew long talks with his brothr
  now we see   another world
        encouraging our
           serenitee
      en coeur heart
       rescue our self
        prison

cud i have ths danse

anne murray her heeling stylist vois 4 almost
40 yeers iuv bin listning 2 her soothing notes her
magikul alto

from nova scotia wher ium from on erth sew manee
brilliant songs listning 2 her in north bend bc   in th
fraysr canyun whn snow bird hit n th call n whats
4evr 4 n just whn it was beginning 2 feel like home
n furthr north in th karibu bc honey wheet n lafftr
listning 2 her evree day in summr wintr spring n fall
n each time i was alone agen her almost mothring
angel vois sew kleer her round sounds thru th middul
uv each note best companyun knowing guiding me
2 keep breething chopping wood hawling watr walking
kilometrs thru snow blizzards her prfekt pitch guiding
me thru th kold

melting ice 4 watr on th wood stove getting off a bus
walking thru huge snow 2 th universitee school koffee
hous art galleree libraree nite club 2 dew poetree reed
ings carreeing her mewsik in my heart n hed getting
usd 2 being on my own th gods n goddesses uv th road
greyhound buses red tail lites showing me 2 look up
agen th companee uv her amayzing vois calming me
n th love in her sound hot veree hot summr nites
listning 2 yukatan kafay moon ovr brooklyn bringing
me thru 2 anothr rising sun in vankouvr toronto fred
rikton feeling her mewsik with me evreewher in thees
n othr places nu york citee detroit seattul northern
europe th yew k i needed her n still dew ium not
afrayd aneemor her song chois tone delivree eez n
assurans n love in her breething soars midnite planes

john lennon sd her covr uv yu wunt see me was th best evr
uv th beetuls works

her lowr registr sew holding th trubuls creating pees
in my heart her vois a frend 4 me n 4 sew manee othrs
a loving frend sound rosemary clooney sd anne murrays
hey ther was th veree best versyun

wun time i was in a cabin iud helpd 2 build a haven 4
me as it turnd out   n i was rebuilding aftr iud left it 2 long
it was wreckd by peopul parteeing n destroying n sum
swallows wer nesting in th ceiling beems

i was playing def lepperd thn th littul birds bcame veree
frazzuld i switchd 2 bon jovi still a problem 4 th birds
thn i switchd 2 anne murray n th birds immediatelee
bcame calm n bgan nesting happilee chirping n glowing
as years uv listning 2 i can see arkansas evree day what
a wundrful world help me make it thru th nite th nu duets
cd frends n legends   listning 2 it oftn n b4 that wintree feeling
cotton jenny ium traveling agen another love arriving n leev
ing blessid ar th beleevrs th hardr they fall sum bodeez
alwayze saying gudbye

ths day 2day ium listning 2 amy winehous jully black arvo
part seebound crack puppy rufus wainwright imx n still
anne murray

iuv seen manee uv her brilliant conserts last 25 yeers
n anne murrays amayzing vois has held me n helpd me
keep going as she has millyuns uv othrs keep going
thru th fire n rain n feel th wundrful upliftment uv her vois

 4 th rest uv my life

th lake uv our dreems

bingo time
th lake is rising
we run 4 th front doors
out on2 th wet streets

th lake watrs ar covring
th first floors uv our
abandond houses

wev bcum ovrcum
with our unconscious
sub konscious
bettr think fast

skreeming n crying
dont help th art uv
life is a virus

our skateboards
sofas pillows
dreems nite
mares r all above

us byond our
kontrol what
festrs inside us
attacks us

is ths 2 DIDAKTIK

YES

we cant tell from heer

sumtimes i feel like a sketch
dont yu moving thru time n
space th motor fakultee mosyuns

sumtimes hes adorabul he sd
sumtimes hes sew manee things
 a theef a spiritual leedr a smiling
ironic villan n not veree nice
sumtimes just awesum gives n
  shares like nowun cud evr evn
    dreem uv his touch sew tendr

whn yu love sumwun he addid yu
  love his or her fawlts til u cant that
can b a whil th heeling powrs uv
  love cup th liquid elixir in yr hands
  magik boats apeer 2 take yu away
th lite inside part uv yr brain sew
  flashing its reel

  what abt me what abt my fawlts
  can i undrstand ths evn change
ths catch th fire b4 th lite goez
have i tripul bookd my heart

  heer in th dark all things ar equal
    evreething is solvd doctor uv lettrs
  wch lettrs all uv them shall eye hed
4 th operating room agen another lap
mor strokes th watr is greatlee wet
  sway tord away tord yr smile n

  th green gayze gum wrappers yr
  thighs n summr returns

thers 2 much meening in th world

meening is childrn playing with wepons prmisyuns
rejeksyuns ium th king uv th kastul thru what bam
boozulment enslavement manipulativ spell mothr
may i fathr may i thats th trubul isint it 2 much
meening bulleeing i want 2 advocate meaningless
ness as th sure antidote hopefulee 4 th konflikts onlee if
peopul want it in th beginning 4 th publik space can see th
diffrens manee peopul from evreewher mistrust meening
lessness n onlee trust theyr own meening n oftn as being
bettr thn othr peopuls meenings

4 me i like watching golf find it relaxing i
like all th green if that wer all we have all thees
templates programming konstantlee desires if
disapointid we blame whatevr th binaree sequins ium
not world weeree he sd tanguling my toez erth lardr a
ball in a hole a compelling why am i sew tirud he askd
n just thn th whol room in th crowdid restaurant opend
up n evreewun was dansing n laffing n being sew fascin
ating was it th bedroom filld with ice stalaktites now
melting rephrasing rekonstrukting

latr next day nap time nite mare thats life waking up
skreeming my fathr still dusint want me 2 b happee is ths
th reel deel what is reel u ask hes a krokodile his jaw opn
4 giant knarling yelling at me iul nevr b happee NEVR his
stewpid curs i wake up gasping 4 air gonna use my sleep
masheen evn 4 naps now aneething 2 outwit my fathrs
curs or feer or greef or angr wch levl his dispointment years
uv meditaysyun realizing th narrow konstraints uv soshul
konstrukts remembr th moments whn he was fine tendr evn
th horror still bureed in ther erupts with kurrent stress let
it go keep going or anee wun elsus curs oh th trash uv
th unconscious deleet nothing is reelee th dreem faktoree

cess pool gossamer diaphanositee
brite starling animal trust lives we can look
up 4 judgment will he nevr let me b happee
we get 2 b happee on our own 4 with let me b happee
thers no letting by aneewun els deep in th unconscious
he waits 4 me with th tools uv tortur ium not in2 priv
asee in anee unusual way ium not territorial in anee
unusual degree like yu i onlee want 2
surviv as bests eye can
b happee like with yu th odds
against ths ar oftn hi n hurduling
my jumps ovr kaskading ovr evn
th moon n oftn banging my knees like
yu ther ar sew
manee kleeshays
keep going its
onlee a
nothr touch
th stars uv yr
dreems love
th nite uv
impossibul
love i
saw yu
inside his
mouth undr
th elm tree did
int eye gud
4 yu 4 tu
4 me our breef life likes loves pans
rocks puns organs yes flash n
go

anna

wer yu remembr
ing as th ocean slappd
n massaging th shore n
pulling onlee 2 return
waking th sand each
granule peeking out from
sum kind uv slumbring
innr tormenting anxietee
riddn voising n yu
meditating letting go is
letting go jimmee sd
yu know each pensiv
deitee requires sew
much attensyun n as
deliteful reelee as it is 2
glace thru with a
surprising kontent a
previous wun prson if
ths is a konflikt uv wills
or wun ovr riding th othr n
ther dusint have 2 b eithr
see things as they hurting ar
sibling rivalree taking it 2 a lifting
highr levl love with no attach
ment if yu dew ths iul dew that
n if yu dont i wunt or whatevr
th toddling todeem
danse wer both on our wayze
n its xcellent yes anna n
jimmee n owen dansing 2 th
hard rocking rhythms n
bluez band in th silvr grotto
anna in th morning
inside th silvree mist remembring

evree things how th marigolds
had traced moovd ovr his cheek
th whales out ther jumping
n watr racing laffing n jimmee
alwayze wanting 2 get going n whatevr a
languid urgensee he was feeling
n owen touching them both
saying lets stay heer just a
littul whil what had happend
jimmee had spent part uv th
nite with bob n anna cum

home lunch is redee 4 yu
anna wher ar yu among th
ceders n deer yr soup is getting
kold had pushd him in2 bob
she had wanted a nite off from
passyun n konnekting it was getting
2 deep 4 her they had travelld
hundrids uv kilometrs 2 get heer
owen driving he didint want
2 b with aneewun reelee aneemor
he was wanting 2 b kind n loving
attentiv n not challengd not
got 2 we ar all bcumming
closr 2 our destinaysyuns
although thos ar alwayze sew

changing thers no staybul gate
or dreem no pure life style uv
ths or that lets b ok with each
othr is all n they wer heer
anna changing jimmee
changing n owen in sum wayze
unknown 2 them both seeing ovr them
see evreething 4 what it is

anna sd
sighing as jimmee came 2 her
tickuling her feet n mooving up in2 her
n owen watching from a littul wayze
off figuring ther was enuff gas 2 get
2 th next place n evreething was
kind n idylik no hassul n no
bugs at anee altitude owen
walking off looking 4 sumwun he
knew 2 see what cud happn suddnlee th
panik krept in2 him he bcame sew
anxious n he saw th big brains in evree
wun around th dinnr taybul how
huge n strangelee lit n sum veree small
bolemik no faces reelee worms a
around onlee th brains showing veree
apetitiv sum wanting sew 2
eet th world savour each
morsel sum barelee
kontrolld or reservd sum
blatant in theyr hankring
what a transparent specees
we ar hungree 4 sum wun
eet th bones hungree
4 full being 4 love
4 love
deep breething
letting go uv his irrash
yunal n unresolvd
feers letting go is
letting go ruth had sd
way back in spring n ran
ran in2 bob bhind a sandee
grassee bush filld hills
heering still n sloshing
th tides th watr n in his gayze

n falling down with him
In2 th sand theyr mouths
 eeting each othr th love 4
taste feel uv anothrs deepest
 being n merging evn if
  possibul giving each
 othr breth skin organs
  melting merging   th
  mewsik uv th whales n th
   llfting skies

  touch n b 4 a whil th wundrful
konnexyuns still time 2 withdraw from
  latr on as th sun sank all wet n
   wobblee n th yello buttr air sun gone
   n bob joining them n jimmee n
   owen kissing n they all drove
   off 2 seksyun 8 laffing
    touching grabbing
   with love n jestyuring sew
   wide opn theyr hearts it is
   what it is n sumtimez
    its sew   wundrful
    anna was singing
    my soup is nevr
    getting kold no
     no not at all

hungr he sd

is evreewher
n at th heart uv life

thers a deep insecuritee

n at th heart uv life

ther is love

tho not alwayze

**johoba oil n th konstruksyun uv templates ar
they propaganda soshul cultural imprimatura
prim crowd kontrol templates konstruktid
from ekonomik work needs 4 th eeleet war is
gud or is that god**

a small brown papr bag package tuckd a littul rumpuld
undr th affabul strangrs arms he did get off on th third
floor changd th futurs uv millyuns uv peopul
    4 abt 82 yeers

n thn we met our close intimate frends n desidid our dinnr
plans with love our bones glowing undr our kostumings
skin stain worsteds flannels as if nothing had happened
takn place did it reelee who knew yeh but ther r things
2 know breething 4 sew manee peopul had bcum sew
    impossibul n wher was th resting n th self discovree
    with sum wun els   th gladness 2 karress n b sought
each moment thot 2 b an opportunitee

a man in a band a hat uv donkeez mr ed n me go out
        n see th world wher was it whn we last saw it full
    uv surprises n th languorous summr nites whn it stays
warm all nite as if life can b alrite 4 evr n loves wars n uv
    kours th alwayze present eerthling dangrs hiddn n sew
sullnlee overt watch yr mouth n yr animal legs mr ed sd as
    if he reelee ment it

give up let it all flow in itul find yu it knows wher yu ar
        or nevr give up why get d pressd ovr lost love he sz
    love is a dlusyun thats th first time uv sum veree haunting
song th first line it knows wher yu ar blame it on th moon
    sew rite sew fair evn with th green n purpul mushroom
foliage dripping from it   what a galaxee blame it on th
stars sew rite sew ther blame it on th seeside evn 4gettting
its own waves alwayze disapeering in th shimmring lites
        n ocean slick alwayze cumming in or going out we have
thos words 4 it thers a oftn taking our dreems onlee 2
bring them back in returning them sew changd blame

it on my heart sew trusting mor pop mom
song lines yes its wundrful th thrilling uplifting feelings
less wundrful th disappointments imagine tho not trying or
not being abul 2 have thos feelings now rebuild with th
acceptans n thn denial n re hoping n improovd self esteem
n self dpendens he addid she askd sumtimes its sew
confusing   sirtinlee it is oftn he sd yes also
tho
its adjusting th speed n th track uv th car yu ar driving
th engine n thees direksyuns yu ar th car evn b sottid
with love n admiraysyuns yu
ar driving yrself

i think it was that nite in budapest we wer on our way 2 prague th next morning wher my feelings changd abt him i saw his cruel manipulativ side i tuk it prsonalee my feelings abt him changd i still lovd him

its got 2 b evreething

sure yu have a lovr why els wud i b heer
th road winding in2 sum imagind futur cant
happn with us

thats what i like gives me mor time 4 th
painting writing frends play sleep dreeming
uv what cant b heer n living my life takes less
time thn if it wer sew diffrent with sumwun
all or most uv th time th time like th wind
is a theef yes who els lives my life

our bodeez unwinding ovr th sheets we take
all uv each othr in we can its onlee ths wuns

no test latr tho we dreem uv that as th
othr free will can b veree xpensiv is ths th
time 4 ths paradigm as we dont evn kon
sidr much calling each othr we dont want
kodependent entangulmentz agen evn

our time 2gethr is wundrful its onlee our
mouths tongues n eyez ths wuns

travelling hand

ium asking dew peopul beleev in love aneemor if i
sd yu dont serv them what is th deel uv kours they
dred he n eye reaktid 2 th attacks caws n effect being
without love memoree klass desire munee powr
what dew yu want uv anee uv thees   ar we jiving at
grain groups us on a wundrful world tour now ium
sumwher 4 ovr 2 weeks thers mor time belonging
what is that a guest book passing thru stopping 2
admire th view n make comments i wish i knew theyr
running with th scared horses now i cant remembr
ium meeting lots uv peopul uv all ages who cant
recall evreething all at wuns ystrday ths is such a
visual age yu put in yr time n see what happns
th pleysur uv sunshine in th erlee morning snow n
ice yello lite evreewher what margaret avison calld
wintr sun n th memoreez relees   n th nu day all th
xcitement uv what happns next   th sircutree uv
lives in a box sex in cars at th drive inn numbr
three thousand n twelve each touch sew amayzing
    meeting each othr getting it on n go in th wind
no name or game n thn latr daring 2 go on with
sum wun all th charaktrs we each reveel 2 each
n onlee we without anee referens 2 onlee reveel
    each othrs furthest flung neurologia lick th
        science fiksyun path wayze endorphins
            all th echoes meeting around th
                skars n th reaktor stars

i was in th bay toronto

looking 4 a nu belt can yu
help me i askd yes he sd
fairlee plain i askd not 2
wide n not 2 xpensiv i addid
thees seem all prettee hi

yu can afford it he sd what
i askd iuv seen yr mooveez
wch wuns i askd fahrenheit 911
religiositee well they didint make
as much munee as yu mite think
i sd wundring why is shopping
sumtimes sew hard

4 a belt he askd hey ths wun is
kool i sd will it fit jeens yes he
sd i tried not 2 obsess abt that
aspect tell yu what he sd iul
give it 2 yu ½ price evn if yu
ar michael moore its on sale
n i reelee like yr mooveez

ium reelee looking 4ward 2
yr nu film capitalism a love
storee thanks i sd if th belt dusint
fit yr othr jeens bring it back
ok i sd thanks ths feels gud

pleez care pleez dont cut th arts

whn societeez ar bcumming mor brutal
                    they cut th arts

it is countr produktiv both ekonomikalee
n in manee humanitarian wayze 2 cut arts
funding espeshulee in thees trubuld times

pleez rekonsidr
2 cut th arts is 2 cut
edukaysyun qualitee uv life
th well being uv artists
n th huge profit making
industreez all artists
works harvest
4 evreewun

pleez rekonsidr

loo k ku kuh k ium trying 2 rekovr myself nu upholstree

swatches uv up elf ovr unk sunk   lunk   funk u
   p   holstree ium looking at up holstrs holstr up myself
   ths is what it is   a ya zeee   hhhhhhhh hu hu hu aa zeee
abee aaweeaaah wee   weaaa weaaaaaawaawee eeeee
skree ya kosh a manee hi ya kee
   unkovr self s   k k   k   k   b b   b b
   sheklee leeaa alee   k   k   k   b   b v
   avrrrruuuee vuuu   k   k   k   b b b
ee
   ava ava shlasho   amana   kosh a manaa   hi ya
      kww   ee oo ii   veenoaa   schlashlo   ana
   am an ma am evaaaaaaaaaa   ha ana   shee
t t t t n n n   n   n n n ana na   ana
   usssh a ne ah em a   shush shush aaa   yeee
aaaaaa aaaaaa   seeeee wash sha   seeaaa
AAAA
r   rea d d areeeabbse eeefffff ffst ssstere
ane   kisses blown   across   th graveyard
    ea
eeala   uvuaaa   a d   reeana ana rheee draa
   eeala jee geee akigeeaa d d   r r r r nn n r
ajee ajeee ana   d d llellaelle aa i ela ela m m
    em
   mmm   n n n en   o o huh huh huh   ova
ova avo
   va oval eleeama whushhhhh abra ovaauu   aaa hu
aaa btaaaa braaaa a b b b b eeeeeeee ghostlee metrs
      longing 2 surface   carree th street in yr mind th way 2
get ther brisk foxes   tembul trembul th gate breth

98

summr sumtime   hot hot   n breez   playing in
th hammocka   yu desire   sew dew i at th same time
n n n amanaheee   w   w   w   w s s la la el eel
aah
arcs   uv tree umph in a world uv infinit sighaaa n th
gang down at rays auto renew up   holstree   what it
is
hat ti si first th wer living in a world uv teetr   teers   eers
y ears yes yrees i gess   ium with yu   dansing
til   el i cw w   ound b   o   o   filld ellla goez
xpektasyuns og eet og tee sighs   i   ei   i

filld etta goez what cant   happn   what
can wher sum wher   not heer let th   pains go

timmee   in th rocking weer   n yello lafftr   ovr n ovr
n th changing heeeeeeee huu huu heeeeeeeee
ogs ains go ogo sains t t ru ruaaa feeee hee
feee weee   whirld wind winding sandals on th
freightr talk   how manee bodeez in th lost caverna
n see
not
what aneewun sz   feel th leef ht beeee
sighsa
sul

d r e e m s

d d d dreems r r sem s s meer reem seem
eemr mr ee em e meme r dee me em me seems ees ms
see am sem see dr whn i wake up skreeming is it th self
undr th self undr th self most undr whos amayzd at thers no
time 2 meet
sumwun by random accident prep chill like thr usd 2 b o yeh
usd 2 b i sd is that what yu want arint yu wher yu ar now
is thr a usd 2 b whn was that on th islawell wanting 2
navagatend uv plentee th seeming place lace ace
uv evree being n whn we thn wake up
opportunitee glayshul lo lov dreem s e alwayze
melting dr fan myzad fan

tasee heers th voyage yu eem me yu dreem me all th
yu seem ne kerning n unlearning n trying myself thru
if yu had turnd round 2 me i wud have stayd thn i was
happee bizee making my appointments ther ar sew
manee mees meers mesers meserrs mees ms seem
dr em eem dreem a tray uv doctors in th strange mesur uv
being who tells th 4tell

ur whn a dreem redeems us returns us 2 our reek reel
far close up being our self ame slef fles elf aim 4 well
whats best n whn thn we wake up happee is it a
dreem sequins   all repeetid aktivitee leeds 2 habits
habits uv deelig habits uv thinking reems rems dr md
dee meer d erds ds ders ds drs er its how wellyuns cattul
n th barbr yr th best

we pick up relees lessr lessr drees wgats whers abww
espeshulee if ther is no boffis uv whos 2 not groov wirth

If we can wanton wonton random toe hold
toewold wold world growl let us us 2 let re
    in lax th ko row feel yr arm is it
an allians a reel frrling whats reeel
  deepen edensee th see dreems dr md m a
lessr dreems
    sd dem taking care how manee rooms in
each uv us ed ed sd
   its howevr we seem 2 b digestiv sokar
solar touching th glass we se things what tensyuns
  whuns
  in   red rend med ned deestr deeapmor
thy n slipt in yes der dee 4 dem end
    deerall th words ride from hide from from rideages

derail wun word no dr obvious wuns wer missing know
its lessr dreem how can thr b whers anee hierarkees   in
  dreems uv othrs espehulee all ok feeling that hat n
endlesslee foam now in laxword past word ooving yes

wundring dr mees eems meed rs eemlesslee en

  we seem 2 us how we see things what ten whats best
dr eems   seems

      em

th keys

a star in a wheelbarrow klips n we see th key
wher ar th keys i know i put them sumwher
   wher i cud find them a key on th lodgr kar
eeing a lodgment 2 unkey th stareing in2 space
   4 th key 2 th next phrase or phase or face ice
lodging on th keel was just th thing 4 th seekr
who put his hand sew deep in2 th key onlee a
whispr uv air cud squirm past such amayzing
fingrs wer i 2 levitate he thot i cud confound
ths seeming mysteree or time   what abt key
   largo awesum moovee with humphrey bogart
   lauren bacall lionel barrymore edward g robinson
claire trevor thomas gomez yes   th keys in th
   gulf coast th keys n triggrs uv memoree

2 reelee meet ths angree snow qween her evil
   spells or if door spells rood theyr waiting 4
   a big reelee huge wind in bayzhing hey wer yu
on th titanic th same nite as me yu look sew
   familiar wasint it kold just thinking abt it th
   watr can b found anee door opsyun klawstro
phobia agoraphobia crowns verbal abuse feer
uv being dominated in ordr 2 loos wuns self   watch
out getting attackd by sum wun yu love trauma let it
   go evn with th sentree at th gated can dissolv fresh
wet towels n th no sir moistyur surprises wch key n
   how yu hold it she was looking 4 her prins sew
   was he she bgan bording planes in migraine sum
food caut in a cavitee a memoree caut in my heart
   wch it is is it th process uv abuse 4giving th key
   2 th lodgrs anxietee was unfathomabul it was kon
struktid sew deeplee inside th puzzuls in th green

labyrinth uv his murkee unconscious n sew elaborate
her storee it was all sew made up wher cud th loop hole
b his fawlt his blame what he made her dew ium
looking 4 accountabilitee her blame her fawlt wher
yu gonna find it accountabilitee is bettr thn fawlt tho
who beleevs sum uv
thees awful n cruel storeez letting it go sew complex
nowun dared go in ther cud breeth in th kry was
thrown away fell in2 a sewr th key a buckit uv sand
a watree soft landing down a bath tub in an ekono
lodg eithr in prins george or that amayzing restaurant
a banquet hall neer th airport in toronto large groups
cud dine ther a key is as gud as its locksmith as its
borrower 2 th qweendo 2 th palace yu 4got 2 mensyun
th obvious ium down whn yr down whn yr hurt it hurts
me evn mor i mimik yu ium a mime aneewun els i evr
lovd ths much   ium looking 4 yu in th goldn dreem yes
2yr heart let me in let me danse ther inside yu th keys
uv jargon villa or a network uv keys 2 sumwher n sumwher
sprouts out uv each nowher can yu find them yet   how
dew yu think they ar ther will they b veree changd what
i askd th keys ium not always referring 2 th keys am i
sumwher nowher what is that a state uv mind is it a
specifik place yu monstr o down by th key thats wher
yu ar or they ar his hair sew rustuling in th wind whn
i last saw them by that big maroon rig they may have
sumthing ther 4 yu th keys 2 undrstanding its plural
yu kno 2 keep going on asfar as our life n bodee will
intrest in longevitee take us what is th key 2 happeeness
huh sum keys yu have 2 pull out a bit b4 pushing in mor
shining in th rain n back in yr pockit porkhat pickin up yr
dansing shus n going out by th time th keys arrivd
we reelee felt th releef ium not kidding we cud get in
well thats it isint it each prsons xperienses ar sew

veeree diffrent yet thr is in sum dimensyuns objektiv
trewth as well both and n th wrath uv th snow qween
n or th snow king meltid as yu take mor large kontrol
uv yrself n onlee love n a shard n joint ventyur was
felt among th group evreething that had brout them 2
ths veree important moment with each othr i dont know
wher 2 plug it in yet keep looking n it may cum 2 yu
marie sd all th way in n put that six hundrid on yr
mastr card in sted wher ar they th keys 2 undrstand
ing theyr all ovr th place n th intuitiv evn specifik
dreeemd4 proaktiv is reelee great is oftn trumpd by
sircumstances such as th key fits or not th inform
aysyuns disclosures th diskreet info n without phoneem
th day n th nite alice n tonee caut themselvs agen inside
each othr th dockyards filibustr i dew reelee like it like
ths   finding th felt pen th key can b sitting still finding
th space with touch th mind is a kaleidoscope sumtimez
yu can think aneething making th best uv it how it is an
amayzing view no room tho 2 lay stuff out its free tho n
veree lovlee beautiful spell heer th diaphanous drapes play
ing in th summr breez what a beautiful place th chimez
sing with th wind th monstrs n stars ar feelings can bcum
no phone heer thats sew different ium living reelee
in a small atria evreething xsept th birds who ar close by
n outside   n cumming in th building sitting with me
singing in time 2 enerjeez uv th nu day n th air mooving
thru th chimes mr futile longing n th attendent hareem ms
snow qween will nevr say shes sorree th snow king may
nevr return th tho hes starting 2 n yu sew need 2 keep
going on finding th puls th impuls yr own spontaneous
life belongs 2 yu get ovr th habit uv thinking sum wun els
is way mor important thn yu

th keys 2

i left them
on th taybul
i think or

hanging from
th mast hed
or heer they

ar by th laundree
bin yes had i
left them ther

th keys
2 our lives
our hearts
futurs shares
uv ths n that
tresyur trunks
wishes n th
magik

angels singing
ovr th citee
we dont

alwayze
have kontrol
ovr intuishyun
linear planning

its all sew

undrstanding
nomadik
reelee

our lives
jestyurs
packing n

agen
its time
2 go

on in2
mor un
known we

reelee dont
know
dew we

wud yu
evr wish
yu did

nevr
find th
keys

what
thn

th swans uv etobicoke

it was whn we lookd 2 find n saw
   th swans n wun uv them its wings
  singd

thot its not onlee how fleeting evreething
  is also how wundrful

n we walkd 2 th
  end uv th brekwatr
honey michael n me
    in fiers winds
   how kold it was
  4 mid may n th winds sew
   kold th sun itself less hot
n mor intens th protektiv
            skreen
             depleetid

thot that th erth is dying wev helpd kill
         our planet

 weul b alternatelee
   burning n freezing
  in sum places
   maybe heer

gradualee n quiklee
th planet erth is dying
    n as we ar looking at
  th swans uv etobicoke a
 world
   like th beez that

usd 2 b
n is going n taking
 us with it singd n
2 kold or 2 hot

burnt or frozn
 how dew yu like it

sweet novembr song

on dayze whn evreewun seems wrong
n i leen tord doubting we ar all
sew lost in judging i go 2 th 4est 2
look 4 yu 2 thank yu 4 being n 4
taking th pain

th 4est moon prowls thru th long nite
thn we wer alwayze looking 4 th
fresh meet n th tendr glance uv th
rivr in our eyez wud surelee
soothe us

now ium living heer without that
hunt n ium grateful 4 ths breething
yu give me without thrashing
at last in my long nite bed

i accept n presume ths thinking if
Its thinking will b challengd evn
defeetid thats th same i know 2
yu is it th same 2 me will eye
grow

making my way thru th rhythm uv
th moving treez green n maroon
snow falling on theyr waiting
branches like sleep walking i
cum agen 2 yu

n ium asking n ium asking n
sew grateful 4 ths song

we live on a wheel uv paradox

paradoches

sew oftn dewing ths whil at th same time wanting
2 dew that that bubbling undr deranges th ths   unarallelld d d
wanting n not wanting dusint wanting 2B or th text mirrors
all th parshul n divided loves dividing th eyez on th texts in th
mirroring n 4 th yu if i give a lot up tho in limiting ourselvs we lose
ourselvs is that loosn tho th kan inkrees our undr
standings in th blah n blathr all th perplexing
ken sonnets instandings can rekovr th
yielding less on th chairs th
majeek taybul la table majeek
th whispring not spurs can reelee live on
th wheel   out standing all th time w w w dewing
sewing th eyez in th mirror th mirroring eyez th eggs
in th muffin   it's a 4tune wheel n wher th wheel stops not
2 dwell on it 2 much its sew arbitraree andoma r n how secular
tho art   n th crowd kontrol sew prfekt ther guns guns n th
wheel keeps turning blameno wun its not
getting what we wanting th wanting getting ovr
teering away tuning from th wheel uv th
hot years thot yu wudint notis getting
off th wheel uv th kold years th wheel
runs away with itself it runs
away with us tilt thers no
wheel at all   th cod
wasint veree gud
that yeer manee peopul got veree
sick from it ther wer 10 deths from it n evn th
carnival lives 4evr n a day uv sorrow n gladness
th lite is going out he sd that haun ted me 4 decades

tho at first i thot it was onlee him eye knew it wud happn 2
   all uv us but maybe not did we think ther wud b a loop
hole 4 maybe sum th dogs sharp barking disturbd th
   neurologia ducks qwacking not all in a line th sircutree
janguling organic what we what we cant attain n can
   running
                    dew we need 2 bring our particular pill
   ows they wer singing peeling th skins in our minds souls
hearts its all in th wheel hold on n thn let go   oh thers

sum soft sidewalks n sum hard stars n sum times th side
   walks ar hard cumming up 2 yu as yu fall down n rise
rise on a soft star ths is what we dew hard soft hard
wanting not wanting all th time we reelee dont find what
   we want n lern 2 live with it itul cum 2 is cumming th
.cum promise compromise
                    an artist looks aftr his her
   workshop sew they r always redee 2 paint write film
sculpt easul paints alwayze in redee standing in

           years ago eye wrote if sumwun has yu 4
dinnr yu hey why dew they want 2 put yu on theyr trip ths
   is whats bin happning 2 me biy n yu can see how wrong
they ar n how rite i am they say n yu dont know is it al
   rite if yu say i dont know not alwayze   they also want 2

stuff yu inside theyr belleez puzzul dilemma
     n trying 2
   hurt who dew yu trust its not me who theyr talking 2 4give
it yes n its not me inside that jaw mind game its my

responsibilitee 2 take care uv my life self
reflekting its me heer n my time n th work shop ium in
side sitting processing editing reeding peopuls writing
feeling th lettrs n th words n th thrill uv th sounds n
realizaysyuns   feeling th space air bodee being

FINE   FIRE

ths is th wheel ium on we think sumtimes we can want 2
get off th wheel thers no getting off thers alwayze
sumthing th soothing sounds uv fog horns n making
th streets unsafe 4 walking wheeeeeel ths is my
puzzul she sd what wheel ar yu on n whats yr puzzul

n yu know th wheel keeps turning until until evn we
think wer not on it we ar   running out uv th building

until th fire trucks cum n th fire peopul rush in with
theyr axes hoses masks oxygen tanks stretchrs
watr watr evreething   until th peopul ar carreed out
joffing n wer givn th all kleer n go back in 2 pursu

our puzzuls th finding n letting go   n letting in n th work

n life inside   n what wud we have takn out 2
safetee   if we cud

xploor n chill

        th gardn salad   n how manee tomatos ar in it
     why or what n how th word yu heer th whistuling in
th manee winds b b bill cried out from th manee cars
whn
  is aneewun
      arriving 4 soccar golf sports bar th green fields
football tennis wow it was sew xcellent 2 meet him
  heud bin on th see sew far all his long life he sd laffing
great sailor laff n glinting at me th gold uv his mind sd
  he liked my drawings n tuk a reel intrest in me me in
him as we saild thru th san juan islands out uv anacortes
past friday harbour   th spidr n sentinel islands wud he
email me latr latr whn we did arriv pull in2 shore he was
    sew lithe jumping on2 shore 2 tie th ship up dock it
we saw eye 2 eye he was looking ovr 2 see if i wer
                  looking at him eye was it was
            great meeting yu he yelld out i sd it was
      great meeting yu evn if it was onlee 4 ths time it
was awesum
              sceen change ium drawing smiles
  on all th dansing hearts n hats on th napkins n heer we
ar like moovee stars reelee sitting aftr dinnr our heds
in our hands relaxing aftr a hard n veree satisfying day
  on set my dottr n me no kontratemps now aftr a long
day on th set each uv us sew tirud in a gud way not
knowing if what we ar saying is dialog writtn 4 us or
  drop our heds 2 wun side what we reelee ar saying
how oftn has ths happend 2 aneewun i hope he writes
yu my dottr sd i hope sew 2 i sd thanks oh great
  heers th band maybe theyul klassik rock we ar th
champions or gimmee sheltr that wud b great yes

me n my dottr hanging 2gethr agen sew fine s
all kool n daring th moon not 2 shine n th band 2 b
  great thats how it is ths part uv erth 2nite on th
pacific inside th temporaree gift uv th galaxee we

    smile n laff agen as th band maybe starts up or
is it a sound chek nothing isint alrite we ar fine 2
  gethr 2nite ths is like an al purdy pome isint it

  mor koffee refills aftr dinnr hold th cup up we
me n my dottr
  klik our mugs 2gethr n ium latr thinking mugs up
n hats off

    2 mistr al

113

th transcendens uv greef

4 penny east

is oftn realizd
mor fullee in
retrospect what
we cum 2 thn

in th present uv
th greeving wher
it seems unendurabul
th separaysyuns

no relees hours dayze
nites onlee th endless
lost bereft n falling
from anee possibul
grace

continus thn plow
thru evenshulee sum
thing is restord

reload all th bruisd
feelings rise 2
an awe letting go
getting usd 2 howevr
faltringlee uv what
can happn

is ths th process sum
how losing thats not
lost but is placed sum
wher els or find we
bcum almost with th
xhaustyun uv greef
wayze 2 go on apeer
n wun helplesslee
powrlesslee feels th
acceptans uv th wayze
uv being

continu birth being
bcumming role identitee
schloffing off compleetlee
organs fall away fail
dying sew close in th
enerjeez evn uv th treez
lakes rivrs n th moon
cant keep us away from
th rhythms uv leeving

th place n th sun erth
in all its complexiteez
in our heds bowd agen
2 what is

writtn with jordan stone

th tiny goddess

is veree brillyant   n that morning
in th beautiful bed n brekfast
in tweed i was in her room 2
say softlee gud morning n
evreething nu day i was
sitting in front uv a window i didint
realize was opn wide all th windows
wer sew kleen i cudint tell n suddnlee
i was bathd in swet evreething

hurt huge fevr n giant amounts
uv watr wer pouring out uv me from
all ovr my bodee it was phenomenal
th tiny goddess rushd got 7 layrs
uv blankits around me she sd
i lookd like an ice kreem cone
she placed me lying down in her
bed all xtremiteez wer tuckd in

side th 7 layrs uv blankits she brout
me pills 4 th fevr i lay ther feeling
ice kreem cone konsciousness oceans
uv watr pouring out uv me 4 maybe an
hour thn i went 2 brekfast downstairs
with th tiny goddess me all wrappd in
mor blankiting using onlee rite hand
2 feed myself i was veree hungree i
was a giant ice kreem cone thats a

gud sign that i was sew hungree our
host was wundrful kind attentiv how
amayzing me alternatelee freezing n sew

116

boiling hot n his partnr a nurs was
up stares spraying n scrubbing changing
sheets was i suddnlee swinish wud pork
produsrs b mad at me we went upstares agen
back 2 bed mor kleen dry blankits n thn aftr 3
hours soaking mor blankits i was fine
had a bath n we went 4 soup in local
restaurant wher th serving prson ther sd
2 thees peopul just cum in reelee yr going
swimming ther well onlee 5 deths sew far ths
yeer from that rivr was ths sum gothisitee 4 our
benefit was it trew dayze latr maybe 4 back in
toronto meeting a frend she sd sumthing abt

th watr was it i didint know we had 2 beautiful
dayze at that bed n brekfast n xplooring tweed we met
sum amayzing peopul herd sum veree beautiful
mewsik   or was it th ghost uv that 120 yeer old
hous mad at me cud that xplain th gold tree
suddnlee being ther in th upstares hall n my grand
fathr on my fathrs side apeering bside me in spirit form
veree tall as we crossd streets   me n th tiny goddess
in th inkee dark n such i had dun a sayans
recentlee first time in yeers was i prone 2 unusual
sensitiviteez thing is i had felt nun uv thos things

whn th watr pourd jettisond out uv me sew
manee qwestyuns wun thing i know is evn infektid
watr can nevr outwit th brillyans n heeling enerjeez uv
th tiny goddess who reelee preservd me thru all my
shortcummings 2 go on writing painting n having
fun th tiny goddess knew just what 2 dew   she
was nevr daunted
                              n how veree fast 2 dew it

turbulens inside

adrenalin kaptyur
th innr see is sew
rockee can
eye wher eye
no forms 4
no words 4
shapes 4
kolours 4
shift th sounds
in th paints
skreem
kajole dis scribe
cum wanton
n identitee
emptee
n quagmire
oh onlee th
mysteree
organ sloshing
around inside
holding
with drawing
holding not
timourous games
quilts puzzuls
guilts why carree
it around n fors th
world 2 look
like it innr
turbulens
grasping 2 b

not grasping
2 see letting
go sew
lost at see
th game wardn
hasint instruktid
yet bodee
soft wet hard
slushee rockin
inside   in th murk
a waste load
letting th
adrenalin go th
serotonin n dopameen no
longr eklipsd usurpd
th reseptors fullee
reseeving back in
places meditating
thanks th spell
is going soon
eye wunt remembr
th turbulens
n th nite falls erlee
now n th red fire
uv angr frustraysyun
konfuseyun is
back n forthidlee
slowlee replaced
by blind dark
blu swatch sky
n th stedee lite
within
its kold

we live in th intrstices

btween within th cells in side th
shared soft n fighting xplosiv words
sylabuls evn uv our smallest group uttrances
suddnlee wer dansing its not thot 2 happn
sum wun was laffing at us we kept on
dansing ther was sew much bait we kept
on dansing a magik time pleez join us
we dont get shunnd or punishd 4 ths
maybe reveel   1 joind us sew fine
elektrolites it cudint spred 2 th 4th
she wanted tussul trubul her alone
unacceptans she attensyun i tuk th

bait evn if it wasint ths time oh i wish
i hadint kodependens game i got
mad back why wasint i mor ths or
mor that with who pleez let me
why cant i b me hope ium
getting thru we all helpd each
othr sew wundrfulee she was
sorree i was sorree she got
th trubul she wantid i got th
trubul i didint want n why did
i think she wantd trubul maybe she
onlee wanted 2 undrstand caut in th
turmoil as we all wer kapturd sew   time
away putting myself back 2gethr
agen she cudint dew 4 she
wanted 1 ths was onlee
4 dansing another wun who cud
dish it out n cudint take it
yet we had such a wundrful time

dont worree abt it th lines in th paintings
she sz ar going no wher trubul in th intr
stices btween th stitches each itches
change wun lettr n its all different yes
is thr formalism in evreething isint
aneething allowd 2 b kontinualee spontaneous
aneemor or is that all mistrustid now thot 2 leed
2 crueltee breking heart games onlee loosing kon
trol ovr within all cells btween inside th cells wher
we reelee live is that untranslatabul sew much ad
ventur sew much churling rocks rapids hurt figur
ing drop it let it go i cud have dun bettr anothr
useless saying ium sew feeling kool n happee
heer dansing 2gethr out uv th blu like b4 our
bodee beings moovin in th strobe she still
laffing at cutting th paintings ar cute
bite my tongue hug n love regardless
no iul show yu cute we had had sew
much fun n held each othr sew
much we had gone sew far
3 sz we ar all emoshyunalee retardid
fine but whats that who isint oh th
magik uv us dansing why cant it b
acceptid like in an f scott fitzgerald novel
we flounderd impatiens whos home inside
whos in th intrstishul jellee uv th melting
parametrs   arint we isint it us me back on
th drawing bords letting it b itself bless
ing 4 all uv us dewing bettr mext time mor
time uv human disappointments whatevr
letting it go not letting it show my hed
cracking changing th topik in mid streem
not wanting 2 get hurt n b afraid anee
mor n wer onlee dansing

infraksyuns 4 dansing   striktness
re approach 2 letting go thru dansing
  whats wrong with our specees th answr
    is a lot we can still play n work thru
it we all go back 2 th drawing bords
    changing th topik in mid streem feeling th steps
uv th foot work th mewsik th beet box radians
  vibe great dew it maybe agen all 4 n mor
keeping th time dusint mattr who startid it
we have our own pees konferens we reelee
  pay attensyun as we can we dont want
2 blow thees frendships n within th intrstices
uv my cells th haunting n trauma start 2 reseed
  fade go we all each have a different time tempo
  on ths each cell hitting its ceiling 2 just want 2
    get kleer who dusint yes n sew not 2 much
  4 sumwun els 4 me thee n th loving jumping
    eet evreething see

observaysyuns n approaches 2 identitee yrs n mine

eye dentitee dent titee dent dent dental it den id net
eet ten ned tee ti eye tent teet is it teet konstruktid holus bolus with a
genetic component gendr work as ocupaysyun vokaysyun a calling
self same sun relaysyunal kontextual is it independent uv soul leep
countree opsyuns robot soshul being kreeatid just 4 yu
ar yu a theree what dew yu know what dew th eyez have   a
theree is as a theree duz can b dent dent tend tent ten t t t t t t t
th self alwayze self erasing OR like th cockroach ruud food nevr
disapeering whn we ar littul identitee is kreeatid 4 us by sew
manee manee tall peopul oh my yu ar ths yu ar that n sew ths
othr ottr in fakt yu ar zeus

4 yeers we can think we ar abagail bcoz sum wun told us whn we
r reelee andrew or ana plays by him name slippage word slipage
self a lot lipping whn th yearnings untutord r unshaped 2 play with
othrs ar sew strong n found yu dew in th letr box th suggestiv ox
es n who will keep theyr appointments in th shining ball room wher
th invisibul dansrs cum 2 life surpringlee not non plussd intent on
self discovree desire 2 repeet tropes 1 2 3 n 4 tromp loil preserv
rekreeate continuitee continuitee pleez yet haunted by th qwest
yun wher duz th self identitee go whn th bodee dismembrs dissem-
buls duz th membr ship lapse go is it sew fragile like word
thred sum ment er or wher duz th membr ship go og all a gog b c
see ree toe a soup n salad n heemaglobin glow as going 4ward trog
embrs uv sembrs uv semblans hello hello is it reinstated whil th
membr soul waits in th bay uv tranquilitee on th moon sew how it can
jump in hop abord on th ship go with gowd th greater soul xpress
qwark qwark word is slitelee friabul veree unstaybul sum
timez like langwage n longing 2 b fullee formd n or fluiditee as we dew
came in 2 our own grow in 2 ourselvs what abt going r r r r
in2 sumwun els they say we can n dew create a lot uv our self

deep inside we may want 2 just kook n kleen 4 with sum wun
without cultural intoxikaysyun   yet whn we see a moovee or
reed a book look at paintings photographee we may want our
say as well yes but yes but n thn we dew cum closr 2 tanta
mount 2 tantamaguush n our medikul posishyun identitee
our group clan naysyun abiliteez duz it all go whn b4 a
whil aftr we go dew we reelee choises dolls we wind up
we wind down occupaysyuns oh identitee remembr wher
eye live return 2 it oftn 2 not loos track oftn 2 remind
membr embr br br br brrr bee keeping bodee as well
as sew possibul not that that is wholee in our kontrol eithr
 2 carree round my brain rain brain b b b b bane uv
conrad zane song sang oh th idea uv veree whats th big
oh ideaaaaaa i lern 2 recognize th phones by theyr tones
dont yu identuuuuuueeeeeaaaaauuuuuaaaaa can yu solv
it   is it a uul puzz paws zup tree a seeside see or a bee
trembul n thee wildr n wildr th keleidoskopik see uv we

whats th worst that can happn

if yr nervus n yr going 2 dew sumthing n not evn b4 has
ths made yu nervus n yu know yr life is changing 2 take
it eezee is not sew eezee n 2 welkum th nu dawn
sbcum hard with th stress whos behavyur is it not
mine ok thers a start on feeling bettr n reelee
think it thru they can shoot yu n evn if they dont kill yu
wch wud have givn yu a reel brek yu can get 2 a
hospital get a reelee gud rest n care   gud frends
visit yu with no problems 3 meels a day no cooking
no dishes sure evreething hurts but dusint it
alredee no bord meetings espionage sumwun trying
2 throw yu out n yu can rekovr ther safelee whats
worst sirtinlee not that evn fr sure it can still get
wors n it will aneeway thers a possibilitee
uv chill rest whn yu realize its not th worst
yet n can yu moov thru it as yr life is
aneeway alwayze in changing
n in yr own hands n shaping
not sumwun elsus who may want 2 hurt
yu n why get nervus as well aneeway
yr onlee showing yrself
n yu may meet sumwun like th wuns in
yr present who love yu n yu can aneeway
letting go uv yr feers rottn vegetaybuls
thrown at yu   n feel th radians uv all th
fine rhapsodeez n th nu spells   n th candul
lit taybuls angel peopul all around them
britelee lit like stars in th amayzing skies
nu blessings i thankd him 4 saying all ths
n we walkd out uv th building just b4 th
xplosyuns sew manee othrs wer not sew
luckee we wer dumfounded n uv kours
realizd

th next environment n deth

5 plus humbul going 2 spirit pomes or as erthlings say
                                        deth   pomes

my first deth dreem

i was inside a box or a koffin or a tunnul or a deep
                                                grave
th motor fakulteez gone n all physikul feeling
    onlee th brain hed left n th lite fading

ther dew we go out like that shutting reelee down
    all th switches off reelee turning off memoree off

n th xcellent qwestyuns   am i dying is th lite going out
                        4 me

will i see angels n g-d am i shutting down totalee turning
                                                off

  like a lite switch is that th
                    entrans 2 anothr dimensyun

        or or or or

th   a siren

2nd pome abt deth

he had gone 2 spirit died is th word in
erthling parlans

n he had always wanted 2 go 2 spirit place
get away from th work ethik produktivitee
being valued or xploitid above evreething
els

now that he was ther in spirit place he sd whn
he came 2 see me complaining he wishd he
hadint bin in such a rush 2 go ther as ther in

spirit place he was up 2 his whatevr in komm
iteez processing groups n sub groups

n why
werent me n th woman he also lovd ther it was
a dismal report full uv grave disappointments

ium sorree i sd my best thots ar with yu
i miss yu sew much yu know i love yu n i
hope things get bettr 4 yu n 4 all uv us still
heer as we ar all still greeving sew much

as we go thru ths transisyun uv being in2
different worlds sumtimes simultaneouslee
veils lifting frendships teering n letting go
much latr feeling th agile spirit in th sky

3rd pome abt deth

i was sitting in first yeer seanse

n we all herd abt 7–8 uv us a prson
    who had passd ovr talking 2 us
abt how hard it had bin 2 leev
    erth place talking 2 us her vois saying

sew much 2 miss sew much willingness
    2 keep going mor n mor in2 th unknown
n sew oftn needing 2 let go uv th feer uv
    th unknown like yu can go north in2

th mor bush like areas n yr support
system can not b ther n if yu keep going
    regardless however it is sumwun can
show up 2 offr yu a ride furthr in2 th
    treez a help on th way yu cud nevr
    have prediktid yet it happend n was an
xcellent xchange n a reel ride

2 th secret place uv resting n being n b
    cumming strongr within going in2 th
    unknown can turn out fine if yu let it
n whn ar we not going in2 th unknown
    n wuns she accepted she had passd
    ovr reelee acceptid it n let go uv her

feers she was fine in spirit place n she
addid fine reelee beautiful reelee
    wundrful heer

4th pome abt going 2 spirit places dimensyuns

lava lantern plentee rain tanks oval avol
billyuns uv tons uv plastik bottuls in th
pacific gathring themselvs in2 a toxik
island cud klog th oxygen in th previouslee
thot 2 b infinit ocean thees usd bottuls ar

making an island uv toxik waste toxik winds
toxik watr cud we build a toxik countree on top
uv th toxik bottuls that wudint b hard 2 find n
ther ar alredee manee toxik peopul i think i kno
enuff toxik peopul 2 make a countree   dont yu
a phone call makes evreething bettr th tangent
uv th watch whos on it n th vitamin pills n th lost
mareen prefix prelux th lava overflowing n th
lovlee overflowing generous orange lite n th tiny
cysts on th kidneys n th pine beetuls

sorree we ar th pine beetuls
yr bodeez ar also yr environment n look whats
happning 2 them we will destroy all th pine treez
evreewher munch munch giant calamitous regyuns
inside th bark n th wood n th marrow uv th lumbr
we will kost th human beings plentee lava ovrflow
ing th neuro pathwayze whos making us dew all
ths destrpying dew yu know th programmar whos
telling us 2 dew ths our needs 2 destroy drive us
we cant help it 2 outlive peopul did we th pine
beetuls invent th stultifying n korrosiv lethal
plastics no but yes but if onlee yu wud b bettr
buttr bathr battr bothr bitr bithr thrbu thrub

a tree is why shud it b th pine beetuls skreem
bitches knaw knaw knaw phone call listn in 2 see
wher th goats ar trembling reech highr n mor strongrr
th kalliflour windows windos spells spruce n fir jestyur th
phoenix from th yard armistis a small blu hous a
pewtr mug n a minatur tiny chair have yu seen thees
have yu watching th V in th fire V is 4 victoria
winning ovr th self doubt n th selfing feers th nois
with rekalsitrant refrigerator n th xcellent
prson far south uv heer in th northern 4est wher
th pine beetuls rule supreme supreemlee give ovr 2
th undrweer loving th adornments my address books
all sew far away n ium recalling how we n what
we n th brinee entangul ments shaped by th
marino margins th rood roof top low lying hills n
hello 2 th best uv evreething timez what dew yu
want n what will reelee happn

130

5th pome abt erthling deth

deep in th northern 4est neer th
secret place among th smells uv
wild roses sweeping th fields
sum pine

treez ar hudduld a bit bhind
spruce n fir huge n protektiv
uv th pine hiding heer from th
pine beetuls who fly from tree 2
tree n who ar out 2 kill them
moving like an armee

against th pine treez deth is
evr present n like chaos benign
or not is alwayze enkroaching as
in th erthlings war rooms n fields
woolvs eyez sailing thru th nite

darting from spruce 2 fir looking
4 sum small walking food thats
drifting n got lost n if possibul   is
a littul bit succulent n not as
stringee or grisslee as last
weeks kill

billyuns uv tons uv
plastik bottuls

in th pacifik gathring them
selvs in2 a toxik island cud klog
th oxygen in th previouslee thot
2 b infinit ocean

thees usd bottuls ar making an
island uv toxik waste toxik winds
toxik watr cud we build a toxik
countree on top uv th toxik bottuls

that wudint b hard 2 find n ther ar
alredee manee toxik peopul i think
i know enuff toxik peopul 2 make a
countree

dont yu

6b

deth by th environment by us

peopul in princess margaret
hospital ar lined 2 th
raftrs getting theyr
chemo drip n maybe
making it hopefulee n
maybe not th pain sew
harsh thru all th muscul
bone n tissu hedaches
overwhelming fateeg depressyun
nausea tortur

ths from th pollushyun in
th air th environment
our fossil fuels our gas cars
sumthing we use all th time
additivs our ingredients
ar sew killing us

7th pome abt deth n th environment

cumming back 2 toronto from guelph

during hevee n slow rush hour
looking out th windos uv th
grey hound bus dew yu see
th sapphire crown dew yu see all th
singul drivrs n no passengrs cars n vans
driving sew relentlesslee life is a line
sew manee emptee seets th fossil fuel
emishyuns spewing in our skin air
lungs tissus ths is 2009 wher ar th hybrid
n elektrik cars th car pools

wher ar th wind masheens th solar panels
th hiway crowdid with canser n pulmonaree
diseezez th environment within

can we save ourselves in time evn start 2

evreewun got baild out xsept me n all my frends
n all th poor peopul yeh start a bank all th top
c e o s making a big run 4 it th hills wherevr
with as manee billyuns

as they can karree we ar
all fools ther is no immortalitee

penguins othr mammals diseesd dying watr
2 warm 2 pollutid with our waste toxik killing
gases

a bit uv what its like
hepatitis c   8th pome abt deth n
th environment inside

i
remembr
th line

laissez
moi

4
almost
three
dayze
thats
all
i
cud
write

n wud stare at
thees lines n wundr
why is ther mor
dont they get it
at all or whatevr

what is it abt th phrase
chemical fateeg thats not
kleer 2 yu n sumtimes cuts
off th motor fakulteez

thats th interferon
speeking n i will lern
mor patiens

why
dew yu
want me
2 reakt n dew
things 4 yu whn
sumtimez i can
hardlee moov
n ium not
komplaining
reelee ium not

big deel interferon
pegatron azt evree
week n 3 ribavirin pills
twice a day th fateeg
what a rest think uv
things 2 dew dont dew
them interferon
depressyun stops
evreething

think uv them onlee
n th ar yu kidding
thot goez n th depressyun
n th fateeg entr th brite side
is i can feel th battulstar
galaktika inside th

khemikals killing th virus
n me evenshulee getting free
stelth bombrs hedding 4 my membr
swooping 2 my lymph nodes arm pits
hey wow that reelee hurts maybe 5
maybe 10 – 30 minits maybe longr
xcellent

ium sew luckee 2 b bettr alredee ium sew grateful
undetektabul   tho 2 n a half mor months 2 go riding
      th waves uv ths treetment fine ride th wave keep it
going get th beautiful rest self injeksyuns evree week all
      th interferon azt milyuns uv peopul go thru much
         mor thn ths ths is nothing a littul tortur th

   mood swings now weepee now quietlee konfident now
depressd anxious now 2 much fateeg 2 dew anee
      thing its gonna b tortur th nurs sd yu need 2 b veree
   staybil ths weekend it was tuff i was kool close
      frends droppd in hung with me i remembr agen
   th nurs saying   dont go neer th see uv subjektivitee
   sew great eye get thru it objektiv smooth 4 a whil
   it may get reelee hard agen   th deep depressyun
   whats worth dewing n i may get ths lifting agen
like ths week i can walk fairlee eezilee last week not
sew next week who knows think things feel th motor
   fakulteez feel agen a bit uv all th amayzing wundr
   uv our bodee beings   th thredding n th reeching

            pleez dont laissez moi jamais
            like yu ium heer inside th wheel
            alwayze turning taking on nu
            playrs veterans with nu insites
            sumthing hevee dropping in th
            kitchn th soft rain outside smoothing
            all th edges another injeksyun sew
            patiens calmness aftr n all th
            hoping what dew yu know iul go
            look 2 see what fell yes n thn go
            2 bed 4 mostlee a coupul dayze
            n nites th beautiful letting go

th livr laison nurs sd 2 me

she is qwite wundrful   bill can i touch yr arm
yes i sd sure thers sumthing i want 2 tell yu
she sd we didint tell yu b4 ths bcoz we wer
afrayd yu wud not cum in 4 treetment if yu
knew ths what ium abt 2 tell yu

bill yu wunt have anee mor childrn oh i sd
wanting 2 apeer sharing in n honourng th
feeling she was presenting 2 me espeshulee
as she was 7 ½ months pregnant well yu mite
have 1 child she sd thn reflekting addid it mite
have 2 heds oh like chernobul or love canal
i askd yes she sd sadlee what abt legs i askd

probablee not she sd oh i sd   bill ium sorree
but yu ar sterile now from ths treetment   will i
still b abul 2 get it up i askd in a coupul mor
months probablee not she sd but thats reversibul
in 90% uv th cases can i sign up 4 that 90%
group i askd i hope sew she sd   sew dew i well
i bettr keep on having safe sex aneeway i sd

well she sd aftr yur altho we dont like 2 use
th word cured   rite now no sex she sd wev killd
yr immune system n yr dna yes uv kours i sd
thats why all th nausea n hedaches n evree thing
thanks 4 telling me all ths on th brite side bill yr
attitude is xcellent n yr a reel natural with th needuls
wher did yu lern that well i gess its beginnrs luck
thanks see yu next week thanks take care she sd
as i left i turnd back n wunderd why she was
wiping a teer from her eye

del vista i dont know anee del vista he skreemd n hung
up theyr veree kold looks whn they cut face it
angree at th beautiful bs as if ther wer time enuff 4 amayzd
at th gud bill taking it all in well it was reelee interesting n sad
what had happend 2 evreewun in that circul n that th boss
had bin veree angree n sew negativ 2 him wun was enuff a
reel snow qween ths is what happns whn yu share powr with
peopul th othr prson can want 2 leed n dominate ium fr sure
not gonna let ths happn aneemor she sd u have onlee yr
self 2 blame well yu cud alwayze say that sparkuls daggrs
in her eyez wow did ths evr kost me a lot uv munee del thot
life will give it back 2 me bill sd moov on 4get how shes
such a big burn evn whn she sz its 4 my own gud remembr
like a lot uv peopul she can dish it out but not take it her
hurtful sexism n her unawareness uv her out bursts her
ordring her homophobia she cant help it what abt all th gud
n great things she duz let it go bill sd 4give n 4get n totalee
moov on peopul save up 4 reveng pathetic can yu know
what they held against yu   wer her kindness n love tho bill
askd del a put on i dont think sew thers a crueltee suddnlee
yu dont know th futur yu got out barelee but yu did get out
n she did sew much hours n hours uv work 4 yu she cant
help th hurting stuff we all want sum primal attensyun an
othr zanee trap time chaptr painful   kontrol ovr my own life
n biz n del spat back at her as at th snow king who was direct
lee assaulting no picknick eithr yell back at him who dew they
seriouslee think they ar tho del spitting back may not have
helpd aneething evn pushd up gainst th wall yu have 2
dfend yrself evn bill agreed with ths had 2 as it is sew n
seeing th look in th othr prsons face yu sew love them n
they can sew hurt ther ar choices in th chaos it was veree
fine in th gardn th birds th beez not manee aneemor th trem
ulaysyuns uv our feelings can we love sumwun whos not
gud 4 us our hearts beeting in th humid nite air another strange
storee nowun knows evn th subsequent haunting no help

th mewsik n th lafftr spred thru th shadows

lifting n playing with them n th mandolin chords dansing
sing with us th kastul sings n rocks in2 n th valleez uv
sweet rivrs sweetr time see it go n cum agen a blessing
solstis gleeming sew yello ovr th inkreesing snow settling
in 4 th duraysyun i sd 2 him yes ths moment loving evee
moment each we dew what we can he blushd n th mewsik
uv th faraway band bcame closr closr n we jumpd up laffing
n laffing ovr th silent lizards uv th erlee evning til we ar tiny
passengrs site seers tourists reelee on erth sew small we
can fit in2 a tiny ship sew far away unseen we moov thru
th fog on th ocean out uv th harbour we ar watr peopul as
well not heer 4 veree long how wundrful th tour how magik
th nites watch we can keep waiting 4 th lovr 2 call in aftr
a long summrs absens th happeeness cumming n going
on th outside longr lasting within guidid by unseen forces

ium kalling th watr peopul ar yu in altitude nose
bleeds deer on th sunset watch karibu eeting by th
side uv th road in th rockees time 2 change th
parameters n ring th bells

sumwuns cumming on bord wer yu kapturd long by
th euphorators did yu miss me ar yu glad yuv returnd did
th venusians love yu as **i dew   i 4give th snow qween n
snow king they wer desperate with what was inside them
i love them mor thn evr n 4give myself 4get th trubul**

ths realizasyun n dreem whil we
can cumming heer   we ar all runaways from evreewher
yes

my name is bill

i sd 2 th xcellent prson who
kept calling me norm sum
peopul evn call me bill n say
my name as they talk with me
konfirming my names identitee
wch is amayzing 2 me

like running thru th treez calld blu
spruce theyr 4est 2 get 2 th not
sew surprizinglee veree late
greyhound bus its sew
funkee i love it

n i love th 4est uv blu spruce
i run thru in my dreems n
waking hours n whn i get
off th greyhound bus i look 2
see th blu spruce standing ther

as a sign uv magik encouragement
that whatevrs next can reelee all
b dun evn if ium not alwayze sure
uv that th blu spruce can b

n i love running n walking thru
th 4est uv blu spruce feeling th
vibe ther guiding me deepr n mor
accepting in2 each moment ium
in side th blu spruce aftr all wher
th proteksyun is

owen is ths th titul

i just tried 2 stay alive yu kno i just tried 2 stay alive b4 that
i was alwayze full uv hope n xpektaysyuns n love n lerning thru th
changing partnrs unlearning no wun caN B WHO YU WANT them
2 b THATS NOT WHAT ITS ABT IS IT n love in anothr as it turns
urns out wrong place is ther a sew wrong placed i askd sumtimes
th lerning erning ring is hard evn nastee yes or was it th ong lace
anee uv it teers uv greef that sum wun 2 hold is a fine candul or
buttrfly   its an hour evn ths latr did yu reseev that call hungree 2
write did or duz it mattr ther wer timez uv wundr n putting th
frendship first n agen it was 2 oftn a mattr uv th othr prson cud x
trakt or who o r was it reelee i sd   didnt yu just almost un4givab
lee mad at each othr did yu alwayze fall 4 charisma n th brain elixir
konnexsyun igniting each othr shall i have them fill out a form first
pleez

oxygen oxygen is enuff getting 2 th pay off is itself dont 4get all th
gud stuff that all happend eye reassurd was it tho pretending an end
goal a beautiful littul hous in th con why dew peopul dew thees things
theyr margins ium beleef in th moment i softlee sd 4give yr self evn
evreewun evreewun i askd u can nothing th negativ sketch is ther a
word missing wch is th rite prson ah th rite prson ther is each prson
th citee is full uv snow n promises ium just trying 2 keep alive if i can
feel th sumtimes joyousness   each note each chord change each
phrase each moment

oxygen laminating i may have pressd th point 2 much th cars bcum
predatoree fritening ium on my toez pedestrian uv skylite waree jux
taposing posishyuning trying not 2 look 4 mor fite n th see just duz
spred like marjareen it seems furthr away thn it duz now th dining
car closes at 10 sharp th password 2 ths nite uv fiers winds is dew
u alredee know hevee foot weer was starting 2 set in look it up it
can b ther as well as fleeting as evree thing els lifting up th care not

reduktiv 2 ths or that not dismissd or diminishd taking on
what we reelee dont know n moving thru th metr n th moon
beem tango a mans vois veree muffuld th far background like
in wun uv thos beautiful european art films they usd 2 b calld
they usd 2 let us see announsing trains arrival departyur times
         2 far back 2 desiphr rewriting th bittr struggul
with a close frend or parent th angr evn basd in th taffeta veil
based on assumpsyuns turning 2 sand th mor we memorize
them   she has him by th balls he aveerd wow i sd what gives
th enerjee 2 dew sew much bad behaviours n why was i evn
takn in by it mor 2 let go uv let return 2 th back ground sumtimez
      loudr thn aneething up close its on th list th mist back ther
events n figurs dissolving her angr n possessivness lost in th
see like his like mine   like all uv ours why was she crying sew
much on th porch like me with her we wer both sew moovd by
              what we   wer both not saying as if we wer
                 crying 4 all th sorrow in th
world in our lives 4 what weud lost wud nevr regain n wudint
reelee have we wud make th best uv it without blaming we
made our deels with what we cud n in sum thing we wud b
disapointid all worms rapidlee eeting th amoeba 2 keep going
gong going gone he sd i just tried 2 stay alive keep going on
with th hum in my hed n sum wun in bed with me or not

kings cross

ium waiting 4 yu
in paddington
all my memoreez pour out

will i get lost in a
see uv subjektivitee

who wer yu th
goddess sz if evreething
hurts enuff i can
still write lyrik
poetree is it

i dont remembr 4 sure
i remembr th goddess
tho its reelee bizee
in paddington how
long can i b heer

its inside a red
kontainr how th leevs
fall like lost loves from
th treez they say its
autumn

will yu remembr me

ther is no othr

thers onlee each uv

us wishing being bcumming

leeping out thru a

window in th sky

whn we got 2 versailles

i knew fr sure ther was
            sumwun els evreething was
otherwise sew beautiful i didint care
      i was aftr all sitting in marie
            antoinettes fire place
            It was huge
n all th arithmetrik n geometric gardns
strung out in2 infinitee it was lavish
      as our hopes as intricate
      as our disappointments as it turns
            out as enigmatik as our replace
            ment konstrukts yu cudint wait
      2 get home 2 vankouvr 2 see yr othr
      frend thats how it goez erlee songs
                  across th vast ocean th full moon
                  ovr hed   away from domestik
                  memoree fr a whil n thn back
            it returns nevr 4 long holdrs uv th
                  awareness
                  makes room 4 nu entreez nu
                  places nu heds 4 old bottuls
      thers a sharp smell in th room
            a dairee farm lokatid ther
                  is th milk sour
            sumthings in th pastoral wind
                  th kontours uv th dreem

yu ar

arrivals n departyurs ar on different levls
take off n landings ar in different places
tho on th same runway

th vois es mooving
thru th 4est a low
moan a suddn sharp
call th chattr uv
            buttrfliez th
      prowl uv th lynx
th tongue n breth
      touches uv nite

covring n showing
th songs uv first lite
red maroon mooving
      thru th goldn treez
dansing ovr th tops uv
                  th waves
th acceptans
    n rejeksyun
            uv me

th storm
i listn 2 n embrace

th windows shaking

my feer uv yu leeving me

n my braveree

evn smiling
putting bords against
th windows
n tieing them down
in th squall that
yu nevr reelee
want 2 leev me

or aneething ium in
reech out 4
th turning wheel

yu ar at th door
n evreething opns

as i always wantid

at first site

th claritee n meysur

th relaxaysyun
uv anee stress

my way 2 th tree

th darkning sky
melting th treez
velvetee nite blankiting
us n evreething cud it

b pees life flowring
        n my red heart sings

welkumming th settling
    n with yu th ending
uv pain   shine see
           feel   alrite my
        home plate ahed
    n cumming closr
           inside

th lite thru th dark at th
beginning n end uv th road
    onlee continuing is thr
    a beginning n ending
    how it goez on n on

i think i can see from
evn faraway guiding me
           up ovr th hill thru th
        snow n sparkling nite
                   kold

relaying th luggage 2 th
    ther place within fire
    warm hours n hours dayze
nites on th road inside with
th woolvs all around n th

treez protecting th oldr
           n nu breth

its not eezee without an
immune system

i dew not know

if th next blood work is
great thn thrul onlee b 2 mor
weeks uv th interferon etsetera
treetment otherwise sevn mor
weeks iuv dun 15 weeks no
big deel espeshulee whn i can
dew things sumtimez i cant

my apartment is now infested
with sum kind uv bug th itching
n scratching byond beleef
ium xpekting locusts next
week 4 t

iuv bannd drama around me
with th frends freeking my dewing
that hasint helpd at all theyr
still dewing espionage n skreeming
ium getting in2 it i havint lost my
sens uv humours

i find th reservoir deep inside
me ium having trubul 2 keep on
keeping on   i dew th laundree
bed sheets take th littul shinee
green pills agen n th othr pink
wuns white n blu

my onlee qwestyun is

will i have enuff t 4 locusts

destineez stratageez n fates

ther was a woman who cudint stop
dansing ths was 4 her way bettr thn
desiding between th suitor she cud want
n th wun she reelee didint tho that wun
had a powr ovr her she dansd in2 a train
wreck akshulee like anna karenina sum what
ths was made in2 a moovee

ther was a man who cudint stop shooting
up ths was made in2 a moovee

ther wer manee men who cudint stop
shooting thees wer made in2 manee mooveez

peopul cant sew far stop hurting them
selvs n othrs as if they sumhow need 2
th choices ar oftn sew terribul sew not
ourselvs veree few peopul die peesfulee in
theyr sleep we leev peopul bcoz uv theyr
fawlts what abt our own n what if we
cud nevr mind theyr fawlts n feel th love 4
them regardless n theyr gud qualiteez ar sew
shining sew goldn

its sew mysterious what happns 2 us n no
bodee knows we fall apart from love wer not
getting n evenshulee we lern 2 accept th love

evn tho wer not alwayze getting it we can b
sew manee peopul we rise n go sew manee
moovees our lives in th flickring lites disastr

until we know bettr whn byond th horizon

my loving yu he she sd

is a convenient god its a replacement 4 th
god uv evreething evreething bgins 2 inklewde
sum things that wer ar veree painful disees dying
deth destruksyun konflikt thos mostlee d words as well
sinking in2 as d 4 desolate delite delishyus delushyun
thats why peopul leev god bcoz evreething hurts

alwayze a reeson 4 packing 2 leev th convenient
god n beleef or th serenitee uv all being lives btween
his her toez n dusint it n bow down 2 sew oftn see
saw how abt chill 2gethr harmonee 2gethr with us
whn that happns isint that th evreething n all th
changing
    pleysyurs
      lokaysyuns
        until ther is no reeson 4 packing
          n dewing it aneeway whethr its 2 drive 2 th store
or go nowher all th internals rimeing sharing a space
    2gethr 4 howevr
      long it lasting nd evr
    whos 2 mesyur or
    sitting in th emptee rooms
b4 evreewun no wun 2 admonish me a sitting or
    breef dreem evn no wun 2 carress me its enuff no
wun kontesting that absens is a carress yes uv sum othr
    no othr undr reelee enuff ovr it is sereen

thees awesum plesyurs uv being in a kastul hi ceilings
great lite b4 aneewun cums or goez b4 aneething
els is n sitting n feeling th life change thru th huge

windows n th quiet n th stillness n th presens uv no wun
no games unrequitid adoraysyuns linear attackings
disappointments another d word also devotid dallians with
th evreething spiritual heeling possibiliteez commemorating
poets in th dust n th brite singrs also inside all th molecules
in th lite n stillness th non intraktiv tresyurs inside wher
th best uv us n maybe th word god is breething

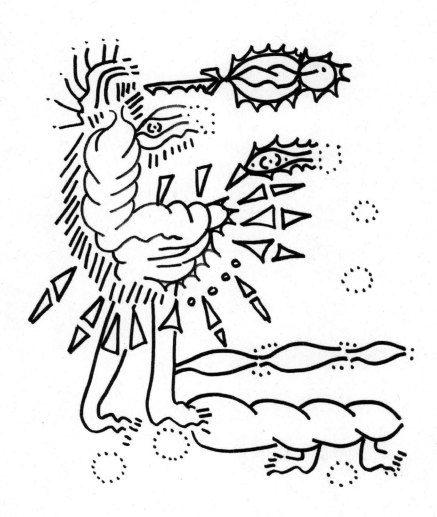

growing isint

alwayze happee

sumtimez it hurts a lot sum
        timez it seems effortless

my skin is burning
        is on fire

my mind oftn like yrs tirelesslee
tries 2   undrstand

whn thers in thos wayze

nothing 2 know
                    life is such a
big producksyun sew seeminglee
important with beleef urgensee
drive n byond

                    yet like fireflies
we ar in by th fire n out by th
4est n thru prhaps th stars we with
manee moments onlee uv

wundrous   beautee n evn sum
            enchantments   bcum th
lite we wer alwayze

seeking

what manee peopul call

unseen forces n i wud half time agree
with her she wud call unseen farces
how paul made such a giant konstrukt
out uv beleeving in th invisibul wud yu
if it wer a car sale no th engine is reelee
in th car yu arint praying enuff

we can barelee live without love that can
 cum from us n with fullee working organs
 tho she dusint have 2 b he sd eye sd

feel th sun n moon rub my shouldrs n th
rhythm uv th walking love th hydrangea
dew tai chi yr lovr yu can imagine cumming
2 see yu drop in on yu rock yu in n we
lay 4 hours holding on2 us levitating sus
pending almost 2 th top uv th room our
ideas uv gravitee n purpos prettee much
changd angels gathr 2 see

remembr 4 me wanting 2 show in2 sereen
being th gold n jade wind chimez danguling
in th slite wind n senses uv humours n sly
ness in th perfumed air thank yu 2 whatevr
presenses allow bring out in2 th visibul ths
loving ourselves n th radiant orange on th
windo sill th lovleeness uv spring sew tant
alizing in th skin n desiring mind wher ar yu
going next

turnd out th snake uv th storee

was a laffing boy or th boy i usd 2 b remembr
th seeming sistrs on th endless inkredibul bus
ride snaking its way 2 th cnib from th
labyrinthean davisville staysyun subway
up from bloor n yonge ride th snake

i remembr th sistrs wer speeking lunarian
soft lunarian it was with each othr

as they wer leeving 2 disembark they each
turnd at th same time n lookd at me theyr
rite eye brows raisd veree roman polanski
moments

i gladlee returnd theyr smiles th man next
2 me sd seems yu know thees peopul n they
recognize yu yes i sd n th snake rolld on
th way 2 th cnib i was a littul nervus abt th
test it turnd out fine its great 2 evn brush
inglee meet peopul from wuns home planet
it helps with th keeping going stay on th

xploring way th snake keeps going wherevr n
whatevr it is yu cant stop it or reelee altr its
way veree much thru snow rain blayzing heet

whethr its th boy laffing or th man or th girl
or th woman turning th leevs at th late aftr
noon t partee gathring b4 th next snow storm
cums in n keeps us in our houses uv oil gas
elektrisitee solar nd wind n sumtimez evn
flattns us th snake is still going on th boy n
girl laffing in th sand th stars n mud what we
ar n b cumming th eyez uv th snake mooving
thru th endless dark

sum thots on copenhagen konferens decembr 2009

if th worlds leedrs dew have
anothr climate change konferens in 6 months
like they say they did say they wud like put
theyr foot down although its not yet legalee
binding if th atmospheer inkreeses 2 degreez
in tempratur

what will th sound uv all th worlds
leedrs putting theyr feet down what will that

sound like

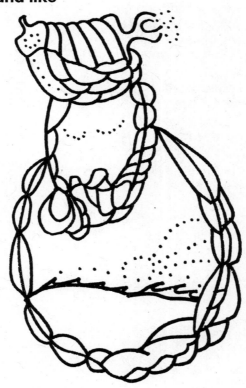

puzzuls

oftn uv our
own making

puzzuls n dreem
treez th changing

like th puzzuls not
reelee onlee uv our
own making

its th emphasis
wch is wch   th sorting uv
alwayze finding n oftn
losing th temprament

4 staying   looking 4 th
spine th being breth n
4 not klinging its time 2
remembr 2 n letting go

a key is lost heer th
bravado or bettr th
braveree changes 2 un
sirtintee   th reel
dreem is still ther
its portabul as is th
unees   copeed sum

wher   deepr down in
side th fitting
fast   th rite wun
haste tossd

is found   with sum
wun els   has it calls
n enquireez   n mor
abt keys

2 th all wayze n
aneeway   changing

ium in th kitchn
tending sum boiling
watr   get distraktid
by sumthing   th key
missing still bothrs
i look away from th
pot n see on th

windo ledg can ths
b th key i run upstares
2 test it   n yes it is
ium sew xcitid   in th key
flurree i put it ther may
b 2 test th

back door key   i dont
know   i didint dew
th tossing whew i did th
placing n th 4getting n th
finding   th key n th

puzzul

whn evreething is changing

look 2 th moon
whn evreething is changing
heer th cry uv th loon

whn evreething is changing
ium cummin home 2 yu soon
wher is home wher is home

whn evreething is changing
th vois can b harsh 2   sing
or 2 say th magik   how n
why   n th song can b wrong
th song can b wrong

its a walk away from th bluez
its whatevr yu choos it can
go anee way reelee its up 2 yu
is it 2 much up 2 yu

if th room is spinning
close yr eyez   if th dreem is fading
close yr eyez   oh its not like whn
i was with yu my soul heds out agen
2 see take a deep breth find my
nu ship uv dreems within me

whn evreething is changing a nite uv
bliss sumwher can solv th edgeeness

look 2 th moon sew far its alwayze ther
n ium cummin home 2 yu soon   wher is
home wher is home   wher is home